TEACHER'S GUIDE

daybook, *n.* a book in which the events of the day are recorded; *specif.* a journal or diary

DAYBOOK

of Critical Reading and Writing

FRAN CLAGGETT

LOUANN REID

RUTH VINZ

Great Source Education Group
a Houghton Mifflin Company
Wilmington, Massachusetts

www.greatsource.com

Authors

Fran Claggett, currently an educational consultant for schools throughout the country and teacher at Sonoma State University, taught high school English for more than thirty years. She is author of several books, including *Drawing Your Own Conclusions: Graphic Strategies for Reading, Writing, and Thinking* (1992) and *A Measure of Success* (1996).

Louann Reid taught junior and senior high school English, speech, and drama for nineteen years and currently teaches courses for future English teachers at Colorado State University. Author of numerous articles and chapters, her first books were *Learning the Landscape* and *Recasting the Text* with Fran Claggett and Ruth Vinz (1996).

Ruth Vinz, currently a professor and director of English education at Teachers College, Columbia University, taught in secondary schools for twenty-three years. She is author of several books and numerous articles that discuss teaching and learning in the English classroom as well as a frequent presenter, consultant, and co-teacher in schools throughout the country.

Printed in the United States of America

International Standard Book Number: 0-669-46436-8

4 5 6 7 8 9 10 -RRDC- 04 03 02 01

Great Source wishes to acknowledge the many insights and improvements made to the *Daybook*s thanks to the work of the following teachers and educators.

READERS

Jay Amberg
Glenbrook South High School
Glenview, Illinois

Jim Benny
Sierra Mountain Middle School
Truckee, California

Noreen Benton
Guilderland High School
Altamont, New York

Janet Bertucci
Hawthorne Junior High School
Vernon Hills, Illinois

Jim Burke
Burlingame High School
Burlingame, California

Mary Castellano
Hawthorne Junior High School
Vernon Hills, Illinois

Diego Davalos
Chula Vista High School
Chula Vista, California

Jane Detgen
Daniel Wright Middle School
Lake Forest, Illinois

Michelle Ditzian
Sheperd Junior High School
Deerfield, Illinois

Martha Dudley
Abraham Lincoln Middle School
Selma, California

Jenni Dunlap
Highland Middle School
Libertyville, Illinois

Judy Elman
Highland Park High School
Highland Park, Illinois

Mary Ann Evans-Patrick
Fox Valley Writing Project
Oshkosh, Wisconsin

Howard Frishman
Twin Grove Junior High School
Buffalo Grove, Illinois

Kathleen Gaynor
Wheaton, Illinois

Kathy Glass
San Carlos, California

Alton Greenfield
Minnesota Dept. of Child, Family &
Learning St. Paul, Minnesota

Sue Hebson
Deerfield High School
Deerfield, Illinois

Carol Jago
Santa Monica High School
Santa Monica, California

Diane Kepner
Oakland, California

Lynne Ludwig
Gregory Middle School
Naperville, Illinois

Joan Markos-Horejs
Fox Valley Writing Project
Oshkosh Wisconsin

James McDermott
South High Community School
Worcester, Massachusetts

Tim McGee
Worland High School
Worland, Wyoming

Mary Jane Mulholland
Lynn Classical High School
Lynn, Massachusetts

Karen Neilsen
Desert Foothills Middle School
Phoenix, Arizona

Jayne Allen Nichols
El Camino High School
Sacramento, California

Mary Nicolini
Penn Harris High School
Mishawaka, Indiana

Lucretia Pannozzo
John Jay Middle School
Katonah, New York

Robert Pavlick
Marquette University
Milwaukee, Wisconsin

Linda Popp
Gregory Middle School
Naperville, Illinois

Caroline Ratliffe
Fort Bend Instructional School District
Sugar Land, Texas

Guerrino Rich
Akron North High School
Akron, Ohio

Shirley Rosson
Alief Instructional School District
Houston, Texas

Alan Ruter
Glenbrook South High School
Glenview, Illinois

Georgianne Schulte
Oak Park Middle School
Oak Park, Illinois

Carol Schultz
Tinley Park, Illinois

Wendell Schwartz
Adlai E. Stevenson High School
Lincolnshire, Illinois

Lynn Snell
Oak Grove School
Green Oaks, Illinois

Hildi Spritzer
Oakland, California

Bill Stone
Plano Senior High School
Plano, TX

Barbara Thompson
Hazelwood School
Florissant, Missouri

Elma Torres
Orange Grove Instructional School
District Orange Grove, Texas

Bill Weber
Libertyville High School
Libertyville, Illinois

Hillary Zunin
Napa High School
Napa, California

Table of Contents

Overview

What is a daybook and what is it good for? These are the first questions asked about this series, *Daybooks of Critical Reading and Writing*.

The answer is that a daybook is a keepable, journal-like book that helps improve students' reading and writing. *Daybooks* are a tool to promote daily reading and writing in classrooms. By immersing students in good literature and by asking them to respond creatively to it, the *Daybooks* combine critical reading and creative, personal response to literature.

The literature in each *Daybook* has been chosen to complement the selections commonly found in anthologies and the most commonly taught novels. Most of the literature selections are brief and designed to draw students into them by their brevity and high-interest appeal. In addition, each passage has a literary quality that will be probed in the lesson.

Each lesson focuses on a specific aspect of critical reading—that is, the reading skills used by good readers. These aspects of critical reading are summarized in closing statements positioned at the end of each lesson. To organize this wide-ranging analysis into critical reading, the authors have constructed a framework called the "Angles of Literacy."

This framework organizes the lessons and units in the *Daybook*. The five Angles of Literacy described here are:

- marking or annotating the text
- examining the story connections
- looking at a text from multiple perspectives
- studying the language and craft of a text
- focusing on individual authors

The Angles of Literacy are introduced in the first cluster of the *Daybook* and then explored in greater depth in subsequent clusters.

The *Daybook* concept was developed to help teachers with a number of practical concerns:

1. To introduce daily (or at least weekly) critical reading and writing into classrooms

2. To fit into the new configurations offered by block scheduling

3. To create a literature book students can own, allowing them to mark up the literature and write as they read

4. To make an affordable literature book that students can carry home

How to Use the Daybook

As the *Daybooks* were being developed, more than fifty teachers commented on and reviewed the lesson concept and individual lessons and units. From their comments several main uses for the *Daybooks* emerged.

1. BLOCK SCHEDULING

Daybook activities were designed to accommodate block-scheduled class periods. With longer periods, teachers commented on the need to introduce two to four parts to each "block," one of which would be a *Daybook* lesson. The brief, self-contained lessons fit perfectly at the beginning or end of a block and could be used to complement or build upon another segment of the day.

2. ELECTIVES

With the advent of block scheduling, more electives are being added to the curriculum. Course slots now exist once again for poetry, reading for college, creating writing, and contemporary writers. Teachers found a number of different course slots in which to use the *Daybooks*, mostly because of the strong combination of literature, critical reading, and creative writing.

3. CORE READING LIST

For high schools guided by a list of core readings, the *Daybooks* offered a convenient way to add some daily writing and critical reading instruction to classes. Plus, the emphasis on newer, contemporary writers seemed to these teachers to open up the traditional curriculum with new voices.

4. SUPPLEMENTING AN ANTHOLOGY

For literature teachers using older anthologies, the *Daybooks* offer an easy, economical means of updating their literature curriculums. The multitude of newer, contemporary authors and wide range of multicultural authors added nicely to literature classes.

The reviewers of the *Daybooks* proved that no two classrooms are alike. While each was unique in its own way, every teacher found uses for the *Daybook* lessons in the classroom. In the end, the usefulness of the *Daybooks* derived from the blend of elements they offer:

- direct instruction on how to read critically
- regular and explicit practice in marking up and annotating texts
- "writing to learn" activities for each day or week
- great selections from contemporary (and often multicultural) literature
- in-depth instruction in how to read literature and write effectively about it.

Organization of the Daybooks

Each *Daybook* has 16 units, or clusters, of five lessons. The 80 lessons afford daily work over a single semester or work two or three times each week for an entire year. A lesson is designed to last approximately 30 minutes, although some lessons will surely extend longer depending on how energetically students attack the writing activities. But the intent throughout was to create brief, potent lessons that integrate quality literature, critical reading instruction, and writing.

The unifying concept behind these lessons is the angles of literacy—the idea that a selection can be approached from at least five directions:

- by annotating and marking up the text
- by analyzing the story connections in the literature
- by examining the text from different perspectives
- by studying the language and craft of the writer
- by focusing closely on all of the aspects of a single writer's work

Each angle is introduced in the first half of the book, and then explored again in somewhat more sophisticated fashion in the second half of the book. The opening unit of the *Daybook* introduces all of the angles and demonstrates their application.

A lesson typically begins with an introduction and leads quickly into a literary selection. Occasionally the purpose is to direct students' attention to a specific aspect of the selection; but just as often students are asked to read and formulate a response on their own. By looking closely at the selection, students are able to discover what can be learned through careful reading. Students are led to look again at the selection and to respond analytically, reflectively, and creatively to what they have read.

focus on critical reading

lesson title

longer, interpretive response to literature

unit title

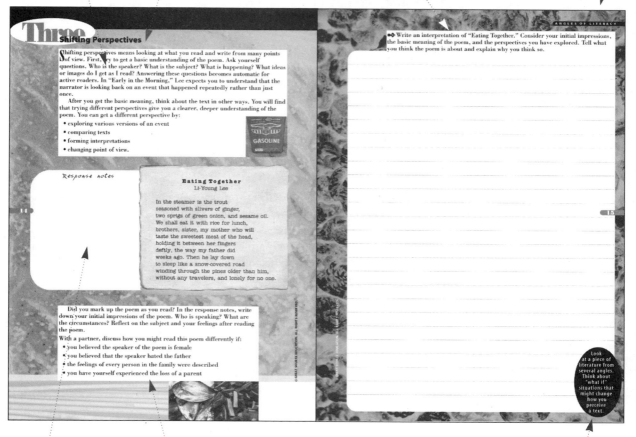

Three

Shifting Perspectives

Shifting perspectives means looking at what you read and write from many points of view. First, try to get a basic understanding of the poem. Ask yourself questions. Who is the speaker? What is the subject? What is happening? What ideas or images do I get as I read? Answering these questions becomes automatic for active readers. In "Early in the Morning," Lee expects you to understand that the narrator is looking back on an event that happened repeatedly rather than just once.

After you get the basic meaning, think about the text in other ways. You will find that trying different perspectives give you a clearer, deeper understanding of the poem. You can get a different perspective by:

• exploring various versions of an event
• comparing texts
• forming interpretations
• changing point of view.

GASOLINE

Response notes

Eating Together
Li-Young Lee

In the steamer is the trout
seasoned with slivers of ginger,
two sprigs of green onion, and sesame oil.
We shall eat it with rice for lunch,
brothers, sister, my mother who will
taste the sweetest meat of the head,
holding it between her fingers
deftly, the way my father did
weeks ago. Then he lay down
to sleep like a snow-covered road
winding through the pines older than him,
without any travelers, and lonely for no one.

Did you mark up the poem as you read? In the response notes, write down your initial impressions of the poem. Who is speaking? What are the circumstances? Reflect on the subject and your feelings after reading the poem.

With a partner, discuss how you might read this poem differently if:

• you believed the speaker of the poem is female
• you believed that the speaker hated the father
• the feelings of every person in the family were described
• you have yourself experienced the loss of a parent

➔➔ Write an interpretation of "Eating Together." Consider your initial impressions, the basic meaning of the poem, and the perspectives you have explored. Tell what you think the poem is about and explain why you think so.

ANGLES OF LITERACY

Look at a piece of literature from several angles. Think about "what if" situations that might change how you perceive a text.

room for annotations

summary statement

initial response activity

Frequently Asked Questions

One benefit of the extensive field-testing of the *Daybooks* was to highlight right at the beginning several questions about the *Daybooks*.

1. What is a daybook anyway?

A daybook used to be "a book in which daily transactions are recorded" or "a diary." Most recently, the word has been used to mean "journal." To emphasize the daily reading and writing, the authors chose the word *daybook* rather than *journal*. And, indeed, the *Daybooks* are much more than journals, in that they include literature selections and instruction in critical reading.

2. Are students supposed to write in the Daybook?

Yes, definitely. Only by physically marking the text will students become active readers. To interact with a text and take notes as an active reader, students must write in their *Daybooks*. Students will have a written record of their thoughts, questions, brainstorms, annotations, and creative responses. The immediacy of reading and responding on the page is an integral feature of the *Daybooks*. Students will also benefit from the notebook-like aspect, allowing them to double back to earlier work, see progress, store ideas, and record responses. The *Daybook* serves, in a way, like a portfolio. It is one simple form of portfolio assessment.

3. Can I photocopy these lessons?

No, unfortunately, you cannot. The selections, instruction, and activities are protected by copyright. To copy them infringes on the rights of the authors of the selections and the book. Writers such as Octavio Paz, Toni Morrison, and Ray Bradbury have granted permission for the use of their work in the *Daybook* and to photocopy their work violates their copyright.

4. Can I skip around in the Daybook?

Yes, absolutely. The *Daybooks* were designed to allow teachers maximum flexibility. You can start with some of the later clusters (or units) and then pick up the earlier ones later on in the year. Or you can teach a lesson from here and one from there. But the optimum order of the book is laid out in the table of contents, and students will most likely see the logic and continuity of the book when they start at the beginning and proceed in order.

5. What is "annotating a text"? Are students supposed to write in the margin of the book?

Annotating refers to underlining parts of a text, circling words or phrases, highlighting with a colored marker, or taking notes in the margin. Students begin their school years marking up books in kindergarten and end, often in college, writing in the margins of their texts or highlighting key passages. Yet in the years in between—the majority of their school years—students are often forbidden from writing in their books, even though it represents a natural kinesthetic aid for memory and learning.

6. Why were these literature selections chosen?

The *Daybooks* are intended to complement high school classrooms, most of which use literature anthologies or have core lists of novels that they teach. In either instance, the literature taught tends to be traditional. Adding contemporary selections is the best way to complement existing curriculums.

   The literature was also chosen to illustrate the lesson idea. (A lesson on story characters, for example, needed to present two or three strong characters for study.) So, in addition to being chosen for appeal for students, selections illustrate the specific aspect of critical reading focused on in that lesson.

7. What are the art and photos supposed to represent?

The art program for the *Daybooks* features the work of outstanding contemporary photographers. These photos open each unit and set the tone. Then, within each lesson, a number of smaller, somewhat enigmatic images are used. The purpose behind these images is not to illustrate what is happening in the literature or even to represent an interpretation of it. Rather, the hope is to stretch students' minds, hinting at connections, provoking the imagination, jarring loose a random thought or two about the selection. And, of course, the hope is that students will respond favorably to contemporary expressions of creativity.

Correlation to *Writers Inc*

Like the *Writers INC* handbook, the *Daybooks* will appeal to certain teachers who need versatile, flexible materials and who place a premium on books with high student appeal. Some teachers, by nature, are more eclectic in their teaching approach, and others are more consistent and patterned. Some teachers place a premium on student interest and relevance more than on structured, predictable lessons. The *Daybooks*, like *Writers INC*, are directed at more eclectic teachers and classrooms.

The *Daybooks* are organized to allow maximum flexibility. You can pick an individual lesson or cluster of lessons in order to feature a certain author or literary selection. Or, you may want to concentrate on a particular area of critical reading. In either case, the *Daybooks*, like *Writers INC*, allow you to pick up the book and use it for days or weeks at a time, then leave it, perhaps to teach a novel or longer writing project, and then return to it again later in the semester. You, not the text, set the classroom agenda.

Another great similarity between the *Daybooks* and the *Writers INC* handbook lies in the approach to writing. Both begin from the premise that writing is, first and foremost, a means of discovery. "Writing to learn" is the common expression for this idea. Only by expression can we discover what lies within us. *Writers INC* introduces this idea in its opening chapter, and the *Daybooks*, by promoting daily writing, give you the tool to make writing a consistent, regular feature of your classes.

But the *Daybooks* only start students on a daily course of reading and writing. Individual writing assignments are initiated but not carried through to final drafts. The purpose of writing in the *Daybooks* is mostly one of discovery, creative expression, clarification of ideas or interpretations, and idea generation. The *Daybooks* are intended to be starting points, places to ruminate and organize thoughts about literature, as opposed to offering definitive instructions about how to craft an essay or write a persuasive letter. That's where *Writers INC* comes in. It picks up where the *Daybooks* leave off, providing everything students need to create a polished essay or literary work.

The accompanying chart correlates writing assignments in the *Daybooks* to *Writers INC*.

Daybook Lesson	Writing Activity	*Writers INC* ©2001 reference
Angles of Literacy		
1. Interactions with the Text	respond to poem	215–216, 220, 366
2. Story Connections	story chart	48–49, 438–441
3. Shifting Perspectives	interpret a poem	179–184, 228, 231–232, 242–243
4. Language and Craft	explore style of poem	125–132, 179–184
5. Focus on the Writer	examine autobiographical details of a poem	99, 143–154, 179–184

Daybook Lesson	Writing Activity	*Writers INC* ©2001 reference
Connecting with Stories		
1. You, as Reader	write sentences of advice	81–94, 105–114, 125–132
2. Reading Experiences	write about personal experience	143–154
3. What Next?	write a story ending	125–132, 167–172
4. Other Worlds	analyze stories and details	134–140, 167–172, 227–241, 439–444
5. Beginnings, Beginnings	write about story beginnings	134–140, 167–172, 227–241, 439–444
The Stories We Tell		
1. When the Subject is "I"	create a memory catalogue	41–52
2. Story Descriptions	make a sensory description chart	48–49, 438–441
3. Events in Stories	explore a plot	95–104, 167–172, 231, 239
4. Story and Its Messages	write an analytical essay	95–104, 106–114
5. On With the Story	draft a personal narrative	53–58, 143–154
Framing and Focusing		
1. Perceiving	write impressions	81–94, 358
2. Noticing Details	write a double-entry log	357–366, 437–446
3. Framing a Scene	draw a picture	168–169, 441
4. Listening to the Text	create storyboards for a scene	48–49, 438–441
5. Making Mental Movies	write a poem	179–184, 242–243
Perspectives on a Subject: Baseball		
1. Finding a Topic	write a summary	140, 241, 392, 404–404
2. Taking an Original Approach	explore main idea, purpose, and style	125–132
3. Developing a Topic Through a Portrait	characterization techniques	234, 442–444
4. Developing a Topic Through Memories	write about a memoir	97, 155–157, 163–166, 227–232
5. Exploring the Significance of a Subject	write a paragraph about a word	95–104

Daybook Lesson	Writing Activity	Writers INC ©2001 reference
The Universe of Language		
1. Discovering a Universe of Language	universe of language	81–104, 518–532
2. Mapping Your Universe	map of your universe of language	48–49, 81–104, 438–441, 518–532
3. Working with Words	write a poem	179–184, 242–243
4. A Universe in a Story	use of sensory language	125–132, 138
5. The Heart of the Matter	reviewing your own universe of language	81–104, 518–532
The Power of Language		
1. Making an Abstraction Concrete	describe an abstract image	125–132
2. Reading and Making Metaphors	write a riddle poem	179–184, 242–243
3. Five-Finger Exercises	write poems	179–184, 242–243
4. The Power of the Word	compare and contrast two pieces	103, 202–204
5. To Make Life a Marvel	describe how you view poetry	95–104, 143–154
Ursula K. Le Guin		
1. The Believing Game	design a book cover	434–435, 441
2. A Story in Ten Words	beginning of a story	215–216, 220, 231–232
3. Truth in Fantasy	writing sentences on fantasy	81–94, 167–169
4. A Tissue of Lies	write a paragraph	50–52, 95–104
5. Dancing at the Edge of the World	write a letter	297–308
Essentials of Reading		
1. Thinking With the Writer	write a paragraph	50–52, 95–104
2. Discovering the Main Idea	compare the main idea	103, 202–204
3. Reading Between the Lines	write a news story	105–114, 125–132
4. Doubling Back	write a paragraph	50–52, 95–104
5. Author's Purpose	examine an author's purpose	50, 62, 67, 96–98, 140, 437–446

Daybook Lesson	Writing Activity	*Writers INC* ©2001 reference
Story Landscapes		
1. Physical Landscapes in Story	write two paragraphs	50–52, 95–104
2. Emotional Landscapes in Story	create a map	168–169, 441
3. Changing Landscapes	write an ending for a story	125–132, 167–172
4. Exploring Your Own Landscapes	draw a map of a landscape	168–169, 441
5. Writing Your Landscapes	write a landscape	97, 106–113, 139
Characters in Stories		
1. Distinguishing Characteristics	write a character sketch	234, 442–444
2. Character Motivation	write a monologue	174–178
3. Character Development	analyze character development	234, 442–444
4. Point of View	rewrite a scene	59–68, 174–178
5. Dialogue Reveals Character	write dialogue	174–178, 234, 400
Shifting Forms: Nonfiction and Poetry		
1. Reading Nonfiction	write a newspaper article	105–114, 125–132
2. Creating an Impression	write a paragraph	95–104
3. Shifting Emphasis	exploring characters	232, 442–444
4. Shifting Genres	write a paragraph about a character	95–104, 232, 442–444
5. Comparing Genres	rewrite an autobiographical excerpt	59–68, 75–79, 147–151
Interpretations: A New Look at Poems		
1. Getting a Sense of a Poem	write a paragraph with impressions	95–104
2. Making Sense	write about a poem	215–216, 220, 366
3. Juxtaposing Texts	compare three poems	179–184, 228, 231–232, 242–243, 437–444
4. Using Venn Diagrams	compare the point of view in poems	140, 179–184, 228, 231–232, 239, 242–243, 437–444
5. Selecting Strategies	write an interpretative summary	179–184, 228, 231–232, 242–243, 403–404, 437–444

Daybook Lesson	Writing Activity	Writers INC ©2001 reference
The Use of Questions		
1. Questions and Answers	write a question poem	179–184, 242–243
2. Simple Questions, Complex Answers	write a poem	179–184, 242–243
3. Questions and Antecedents	analyze a stanza of a poem	179–184, 228, 231–232, 242–243, 437–446
4. Questions and Similes	write a poem using a simile	138, 179–184, 236, 242–243
5. Questions and Paradoxes	compare writing and sketching	103, 202–204
Writing from Models		
1. Spinoff Modeling	write a poem	179–184, 242–243
2. Description Through Detail	write a "where I'm from" poem	179–184, 242–243
3. Repetition	write a description	97, 106–113, 139
4. Extended Metaphor	write a poem	179–184, 242–243
5. Word-for-Word Modeling	write an emulation	92, 179–184, 242–243
Rudolfo Anaya		
1. Finding a Voice	create a chart	48–49, 438–441
2. The Importance of the Past	write a short essay	95–104, 106–114
3. The Importance of Values	write a short analytical essay	95–104, 106–114
4. The Art of Storytelling	write a paragraph	50–52, 95–104
5. Finding a Style	write a letter	297–308

Angles of Literacy

by Louann Reid

When we view something of potential value, such as a diamond or an antique vase, we often examine it from all sides. We hold it up and slowly turn it, looking first at the front, then the sides and back. Combining information from each perspective, we construct a fuller picture of the object and its worth.

Similarly, we can examine a concept or idea from several angles, or perspectives, using a variety of approaches to understand a complex concept. Perhaps no concept in education is more complex—or more important—than literacy.

"Literacy" is frequently defined as the ability to read and write. But people also need to be able to read critically, write effectively, draw diagrams, collaborate with others, listen carefully, and understand complex instructions. In short, literacy means being able to do whatever is required to communicate effectively in a variety of situations. Angles of Literacy is the term we use in these *Daybooks* to identify five approaches to becoming literate.

THE FIVE ANGLES

The Angles of Literacy are major perspectives from which to examine a text. Strategies within each angle further define each one. Activities in the *Daybooks* provide students with multiple opportunities to become autonomous users of the strategies on other literature that they will encounter.

The angles are listed on page seven in an order that reflects the way that readers and writers first engage with the text. They are encouraged to move gradually from that initial engagement to a more evaluative or critical stance where they study the author's language and craft, life and work. They critique the texts they read and consider what other critics have written. Moving from engagement through interpretation to evaluation is the process that Louise Rosenblatt and later reader-response critics advocate.

In our own work with secondary school students, we have repeatedly seen the value of encouraging students to read and write using all three stages—engagement, interpretation, evaluation. We also know that students sometimes begin at a different stage in the process—perhaps with interpretation rather than engagement. So, our five angles are not meant to be a hierarchy. Students may begin their engagement with the text using any angle and proceed in any order. Depending on the text and the context, readers might start with making personal connections to the stories in an essay. If the text is by an author that the students know well, they might naturally begin by comparing this work to the author's other works.

STRATEGIES

Strategies are plans or approaches to learning. By using some strategies over and over, students can learn to comprehend any text. The *Daybook* activities, such as annotating or visualizing a specific poem, story, or essay, provide students multiple opportunities to develop these strategies. From using this scaffolding students gradually become more independent readers and, ultimately, fully literate.

Because strategies are employed through activities, it may seem at first that they are the same thing. Yet, it is important to remember that a strategy is a purposeful plan. When, as readers, we select a strategy such as underlining key phrases, we have selected this action deliberately to help us differentiate between important information and unimportant information. We may use a double-entry log (an activity) to identify the metaphors in a poem. Our purpose in doing so is to understand figurative language (a strategy). Strategies are purposeful plans, often consisting of one or more activities, to help us comprehend and create.

At the end of each lesson, the strategies are explicitly stated. In a sentence or two, the main point of the activity is noted. When students complete all 80 lessons in a daybook, they will have 80 statements of what they, as active readers, can do to read critically and write effectively.

Reflection is a vital component in helping students understand the use of strategies. After using a particular strategy, students need to step back and consider how the strategy worked or did not. They might think about how an approach or a strategy can change their understanding of what they read and write. Students might ask themselves a series of questions such as: What have I done? What have I learned? What would I do differently next time? How did the angle or strategy affect my understanding? What would I understand differently if I had changed the angle or the strategy?

ACTIVITIES

Each lesson in these *Daybooks* contains activities for students. From rereading to discussing with a partner to making a story chart, students learn how to become better critical readers and more effective writers. Many activities encourage students to write to learn. Other activities encourage students to increase their understanding of a text by visualizing it in a sketch or a graphic organizer. But, as much as possible, the *Daybooks* try to encourage students to make a creative written response with a poem, some dialogue, a character sketch, or some other creative assignment.

We have selected activities that work particularly well with the texts in the lesson and with the strategies we want students to develop. However, as you will see when you and your students use the *Daybooks*, there are several possible activities that could reinforce a particular strategy. You may want to have students try some of these activities, such as making a story chart or using a double-entry log, when they read other texts in class. This would also be another opportunity to have students ask themselves the reflective questions.

Angles of Literacy

ANGLE OF VISION	STRATEGIES	SELECTED ACTIVITIES
Interacting with a Text	• underlining key phrases • writing questions or comments in the margin • noting word patterns and repetitions • circling unknown words • keeping track of the story or idea as it unfolds	• Write down initial impressions. • Re-read. • Write a summary of the poem. • Generate two questions and one "certainty." Then, discuss the questions and statement in a small group.
Making Connections to the Stories within a Text	• paying attention to the stories being told • connecting the stories to one's own experience • speculating on the meaning or significance of incidents	• Make a story chart with three columns—incident in the poem, significance of the incident, related incident in my life. • Write a news story of events behind the story in the poem.
Shifting Perspectives to Examine a Text from Many Points of View	• examining the point of view • changing the point of view • exploring various versions of an event • forming interpretations • comparing texts • asking "what if" questions	• Discuss with a partner or small group how you might read a poem differently if: 　　the speaker was female 　　you believe the speaker is a parent. • Rewrite the text from a different point of view.
Studying the Language and Craft of a Text	• understanding figurative language • looking at the way the author uses words • modeling the style of other writers • studying various kinds of literature	• Use a double-entry log to identify metaphors and the qualities implied by the comparison. • Examine the title of the poem and its relationship to the text.
Focusing on the Writer's Life and Work	• reading what the author says about the writing • reading what others say • making inferences about the connections between an author's life and work • analyzing the writer's style • paying attention to repeated themes and topics in the work by one author	• Read about the poet's life. Then make an inference chart to record evidence from the poet's life, an inference, a comparison to the poem. • Write an evaluation of the poem. Then, read what one or more critics have said about the poem or poet. Finally, write a short response, either agreeing or disagreeing with the critic. Support your ideas with textual evidence.

Responding to Literature Through Writing
by Ruth Vinz

We have found that students' encounters with literature are enriched when they write their way toward understanding. The writing activities in the *Daybooks* are intended to help students explore and organize their ideas and reactions during and after reading. We try to make use of the exploratory and clarifying roles of writing through various activities.

Exploratory assignments include those through which students question, analyze, annotate, connect, compare, personalize, emulate, map, or chart aspects in the literary selections. Generally these assignments aid students' developing interpretations and reactions to the subjects, themes, or literary devices in the literature they are reading. Other writing activities offer students the opportunity to clarify their understanding of what they've read. These assignments lead students to look at other perspectives, determine the significance of what they read, and prioritize, interpret, question, and reflect on initial impressions. Further, students are asked to create literature of their own as a way of applying the concepts they're learning. Writing to clarify also involves students in reflection, where they are asked to think about their reactions and working hypotheses. Taken together, the writing activities represent a series of strategies that students can apply to the complex task of reading literature.

The writing activities included in the *Daybooks* start students on the path toward understanding. We did not take it as the function of the writing activities in this book to lead students through the writing process toward final, finished drafts. Although examples of extensions are included here in the Teacher's Guide, the writing in the *Daybooks* introduces first draft assignments that may lead into more formal writing if you, as the teacher, so choose.

You will have your own ideas about assisting students with the writing activities or extending the writing beyond the *Daybooks*. We think it's important for you to remind students that the writing in which they engage is useful for their reading outside the *Daybooks*. For example, students may use various types of maps, charts, or diagrams introduced in the *Daybooks* when they read a novel. They may find that the response notes become a strategy they use regularly. Once exposed to imitation and modeling, students may find these useful tools for understanding an author's style, language or structure. If your students develop a conscious awareness of the strategies behind the particular writing activities, they can apply these in other reading situations.

Writing assignments to explore and to clarify students' developing interpretations are incorporated in two types of activities, both of which are elaborated on below.

WRITING ABOUT LITERATURE

You will find activities in every cluster of lessons that call upon students to write about the literature they are reading. We developed these writing assignments to help facilitate, stimulate, support, and shape students' encounters with literature. We think the assignments have four purposes:

(1) to connect the literature to the students' personal experiences; (2) to re-examine the text for various purposes (language and craft, connections with other texts, shifting perspectives, developing interpretations); (3) to develop hypotheses, judgments, and critical interpretations; (4) to apply the idea behind the lesson to a new literary text or situation.

The types of writing we have used to fulfill these purposes are:

1. Response Notes Students keep track of their initial responses to the literature by questioning, annotating, and marking up the text in various ways. The response notes are used to get students in the habit of recording what they are thinking while reading. Seldom do we begin by telling them what and how to write in this space. Many times we circle back and ask them to build on what they have written with a particular focus or way of responding. In the response notes, students are encouraged to make personal connections, re-examine text, jot down ideas for their own writing, and monitor their changing responses.

2. Personal Narrative Students write personal stories that connect or relate to what they have read. In some cases, the narratives tell the stories of students' prior reading experiences or how a literary selection relates to their life experiences. Other activities use personal narrative to apply and refine students' understanding of narrative principles.

3. Idea Fund Students collect ideas for writing—catalogs, lists, charts, clusters, diagrams, double-entry logs, sketches, or maps. These forms of idea gathering are useful for analyzing particular literary selections and will aid the initial preparation for longer pieces of critical analysis.

4. Short Response Students write summaries; paraphrase main themes or ideas; and compose paragraphs of description, exposition, explanation, evaluation, and interpretation.

5. Analysis Students write short analyses that take them beyond summarizing the literary selection or their personal reactions to it. The analytic activities engage students in recognizing symbols and figures of speech and the links between events, characters, or images. Again, these short analytical responses are intended to prepare students for longer, critical interpretation that you, as a teacher, might assign.

6. Speculation Students' speculations are encouraged by writing activities that engage them in predicting, inferring, and imagining. "What if. . .," "How might. . .," and "Imagine that. . ." are all ways in which students are invited to see further possibilities in the literature they read.

Students use writing to record and reflect on their reactions and interpretations. At times, students are asked to share their writing with others. Such sharing is another form of reflection through which students have an opportunity to "see again" their own work in the context of what others have produced.

The writing activities in the *Daybooks* will help students connect what they read with what they experience and with what they write, and also to make connections between the literary selections and literary techniques. The activities encourage students to experiment with a range of forms, choose a range of focuses, and reflect on what they have learned from these. We hope the writing serves to give students access to a kind of literary experience they can value and apply in their future reading.

WRITING LITERATURE

Within a literary work, readers find a writer's vision, but readers also co-create the vision along with the writer and learn from his or her craft. We've asked our students to write literature of their own as a way of responding to what they read. Through writing literature, students can explore facets of the original work or use the techniques of a variety of authors. Here are a number of the activities introduced in the *Daybooks*:

1. Take the role of writer Students write imaginative reconstructions of gaps in a text by adding another episode, adding dialogue, rewriting the ending, adding a section before or after the original text, adding characters, changing the setting, or creating dream sequences. Such imaginative entries into the text require that students apply their knowledge of the original.

2. Imitation and Modeling The idea of modeling and imitation is not new. Writers learn from other writers. The modeling activities are intended to help students "read like a writer." In these activities, students experiment with nuances of expression, syntactic and other structural principles, and apply their knowledge of literary devices (for example, *rhythm, imagery, metaphor*). One goal in educating students with literature is to make explicit what writers do. One way to achieve the goal is to provide models that illustrate various principles of construction.

3. Original Pieces Students write poems, character sketches, monologues, dialogues, episodes, vignettes, and descriptions as a way to apply the knowledge about language and craft they are gaining through their reading.

4. Living Others' Perspectives Writing from others' points of view encourages students to step beyond self to imagine other perspectives. Students write from a character's point of view, compose diary entries or letters, explain others' positions or opinions, and other reactions to a situation. These writing activities encourage students to explore the concerns of others and to project other perspectives through their writing.

The writing becomes a record of students' developing and changing ideas about literature. By the time students have finished all of the writing in this book, they will have used writing strategies that can assist them in all future reading.

Reading, Writing, and Assessment
by Fran Claggett

As teachers, we all cope with the complexities of assessing student performance. We must be careful readers of student work, attentive observers of student participation in various activities, and focused writers in responding to student work. We must understand the value of rewarding what students do well and encouraging them to improve. Above all, we need to make the criteria for assessment clear to students.

THE DAYBOOKS

The *Daybooks* provide visible accounts of many aspects of the reading process. Students record all the various permutations of active reading and writing. In the current view of most teachers and researchers, reading is a process of constructing meaning through transactions with a text. In this view, the individual reader assumes responsibility for interpreting a text guided not only by the language of the text but also by the associations, cultural experiences, and prior knowledge that the reader brings to the interpretive task. Meaning does not reside solely within the words on the page. Our view of reading emphasizes the role of the reader. Construction of meaning, rather than the gaining and displaying of knowledge should be the goal of reading instruction. This rule is reflected throughout the *Daybooks*, which guide students in how to read, respond to, interpret, and reflect on carefully selected works of literature.

Within these lessons, students interact with a text from five angles of literacy. The *Daybooks* make it possible for both students and teachers to track students' increasing sophistication in using the angles to make sense of their reading. Through the strategies presented in the lessons, students learn to express their understanding of a text. They will do such things as show their understanding of figurative language and the importance of form; write about how characters are developed and change; and demonstrate their understanding of how a piece of literature develops.

THE ROLE OF THE TEACHER

The teacher is critical to the *Daybook* agenda. Conceivably, a teacher could pass out the *Daybooks* and turn the students loose, but that would not result in the carefully guided reading and writing that is intended. Rather, the teachers are central to student success. Because of the format of the *Daybooks*, lessons are short, each taking no more than a normal class period. They are intended to be complete in themselves, yet most teachers will see that there are numerous opportunities for extensions, elaborations, further readings, group work, and writing. The Teacher's Guide provides some suggestions; you will think of many others. The *Daybooks* offer guidelines for reading and thinking, for writing and drawing used in the service of reading. They also provide many opportunities for students to write pieces of their own, modeling, responding, interpreting, and reflecting on the pieces that they have read. Many of these pieces might lead to later revision, refining, group response, and editing. It is the teacher, however, who knows the students well enough to see which pieces would be worthwhile to work with and which it is best to leave as exercises rather than completed works.

In assessing the *Daybooks*, it is important to remember to look at the students growing facility with the processes of reading. As is true with all learning, there will be false starts, abandoned practices, and frustrations, yet also illuminations, progress, and occasional epiphanies. No music teacher ever graded every attempt at mastering a piece of music. We, too, must resist the urge—honed by years of assessing only products or finished papers—of overassessing the *Daybooks*. We must consider them the place where students are free to think things through, change their minds, even start over. But you can be alert to what the student is doing well, what is frustrating, what needs more time. To that end, we have provided a chart which may be useful in getting a sense of how students are progressing in using angles of literacy. By duplicating the chart for each student, you can track progress through the lessons. We would like to encourage the idea of jotting down notations as you work with students during the class period or look over the *Daybooks* after class. In this way, you can amass a sizable amount of information over a grading period. Coupled with a student self-assessment such as the one included here, you will have tangible evidence of achievement in the *Daybooks*.

STUDENT SELF-ASSESSMENT

A student self-assessment chart is a useful adjunct to the teacher chart. This particular format works well as it asks students to consider interest, value, and participation as well as quality.

Followed by the self-assessment essay, it provides valuable insight into the student's sense of accomplishment.

INDIVIDUAL STUDENT EIGHT-WEEK ASSESSMENT CHART

The columns for each week's lessons can be used in different ways. We suggest the number system: a 5 for insightful, imaginative thinking or responding, a 1 for a minimal attempt. Some teachers prefer the check, check-plus, check-minus system. There is even room, if you turn the chart sideways, to make some notations.

Angles of Literacy

INTERACTING WITH A TEXT	I	II	III	IV	V	VI	VII	VIII
The student demonstrates understanding by using interactive strategies such as:								
underlining key phrases								
writing questions or comments in the margin								
noting word patterns and repetitions								
circling unknown words								
keeping track of ideas as they unfold								

MAKING CONNECTIONS	I	II	III	IV	V	VI	VII	VIII
The student makes connections to the stories with a text by:								
paying attention to the stories in the text								
connecting ideas and themes in the text to personal ideas, experience, feelings, and knowledge								
making connections to other texts, movies, television shows, or other media								

SHIFTING PERSPECTIVES	I	II	III	IV	V	VI	VII	VIII
The student is able to shift perspectives to examine a text from many points of view. When prompted, the student will engage in such strategies as these:								
examine the point of view								
change the point of view								
explore various versions of an event, form interpretations								
compare texts, and respond to "what if" questions to deepen understanding								

STUDYING THE LANGUAGE AND CRAFT OF A TEXT	I	II	III	IV	V	VI	VII	VIII

The student will demonstrate an understanding of the way language and craft operate in a text. Specifically, the student will show how:

imagery, metaphor, and figurative language are central to literature

demonstrate an understanding of how an author's vocabulary and use of language are integral to the overall work

use modeling to demonstrate an understanding of style and form

demonstrate understanding of various genres and forms of literature

INTERACTING WITH A TEXT	I	II	III	IV	V	VI	VII	VIII

The student will demonstrate a rich understanding of a single writer's work, including:

interpreting short texts by the author

making inferences about the connections between an author's life and work

analyzing the writer's style

drawing conclusions about repeated themes and topics in an author's work

evaluating a text or comparing works by the same author

END OF TERM STUDENT SELF-ASSESSMENT CHART

Fill out the chart by naming or describing the work you have completed in the *Daybooks*. Since the *Daybooks* are focused on the reading of and writing about literature, it might be useful to list the actual texts you have read. To measure your achievement, think about the work you did as you explored the angles of vision for each text.

For each item, use the numbers 1 (low) to 5 (high) to indicate the four **aspects of your involvement. Following completion of the chart, write the Self-Assessment Essay.**

WORKS OF LITERATURE READ	LEVEL OF INTEREST	LEVEL OF VALUE	DEGREE OF PARTICIPATION	QUALITY OF PARTICIPATION

STUDENT SELF-ASSESSMENT ESSAY

After you have filled out this chart, write a self-evaluation essay reflecting on your work in the *Daybooks* for the past term and articulating ideas about what you hope to achieve in the next. Refer specifically to the texts listed in the chart, elaborating on your assessment of a text's interest or value; commenting on reasons for the degree of your involvement or explaining why you have assessed the quality of your work as you have.

Modeling: An Overview
by Fran Claggett

The overriding goal in modeling is to help students become discerning readers and inventive, perceptive writers. Modeling works well with students of all ability levels, whether homogeneously or heterogeneously grouped. It is especially effective in working with second-language students. My own classroom experience, as well as testimony from writers and researchers, indicates that modeling closely resembles the natural stages we go through in the acquisition of language. Many writers have talked about how, during their formative years, they either consciously or unconsciously imitated the styles of other writers whom they admired. Here, I will focus on the metacognitive aspects of modeling, making the processes of thinking and learning explicit for students, urging them to explore their own ways of making sense not only of what they read but what they write.

USING MODELING IN THE CLASSROOM

Through various modeling experiences, students learn the relationships among form, structure, and style. They learn to slow down their reading in order to appreciate the ways authors create specific effects. A critical aspect of using modeling with all students is the selection of the work to be modeled. The teacher must be clear on the focus of the assignment, allow for the margin of success by selecting works for modeling that are within the student's grasp, and make certain that students enter into the metacognitive aspect of the exercise.

Some of the ways that modeling can be integrated into classroom assignments:

1. As a catalyst for writing, particularly for reluctant writers. It immediately provides a structure and takes away much of the threat of the blank page.

2. As an introduction to poetry. Again, much of the onus is gone when students first model a poem, then discover the form by analyzing their own work as well as the original.

3. To encourage close reading of a text. As part of the study of a novel—particularly a difficult one stylistically—have students choose a representative passage (they decide what is representative), model it, then do a structural analysis of it. This exercise enhances both their understanding of the content of the original (it slows down their reading) and their grasp of the author's style. Students often work together in pairs or groups on this activity.

4. To teach awareness of diction. Choose a passage and, as a class, analyze its tone by exploring the use of diction, detail, and syntax. They might even write an analysis of the passage. Either after or before the analysis, students choose a different subject from that of the original and emulate the passage, working consciously to create a particular tone or effect. Students can also write emulations of each other's work, accompanied by an analysis and critique.

5. As a way of teaching English language sentence patterns to second-language learners. By modeling, students are able to internalize the natural flow of English sentences.

6. As part of an intensive author study. Students read a variety of works (short stories, essays, poems, novels, plays) by a single author. They select sections they believe to be representative of the author's style and analyze them from the standpoint of diction, tone, and main idea. They should model a short section. Their final piece in this assignment, which also involves secondary source

biographical research, is to write a full imitation of the style of this author, showing through their choice of subject matter, genre, syntax, voice, and tone that they have developed and internalized a familiarity with the author's style.

KINDS OF MODELING TAUGHT IN THE DAYBOOKS

Emulation	replace word for word by function
Spinoff Modeling	respond to original content; retain tone, perhaps first line
Fixed Form Modeling	follow the pattern or form of the original (e.g., a sonnet)
Structural Modeling	model the thought progressions of the original
The Paralog	create a parallel dialogue with the author
Style Modeling	write a substantial piece in the style of an author

Unit Overview

In this unit, students will explore some of the many different ways readers can respond to a text. Critical readers know that they need to read actively. They need to highlight and mark a text, pay attention to the various perspectives of a text, and consider the language, structure, and style of the writing. In addition, they need to understand how the author's experiences and ideas can affect the meaning and context of a text.

LITERATURE FOCUS

Lesson	*Literature*
1. Interactions with the Text	**Li-Young Lee,** "Early in the Morning" (Poetry) **Li-Young Lee,** "The Gift" (Poetry)
2. Story Connections	
3. Shifting Perspectives	**Li-Young Lee,** "Eating Together" (Poetry)
4. Language and Craft	**Li-Young Lee,** "Mnemonic" (Poetry)
5. Focus on the Writer	**Li-Young Lee,** from *The Winged Seed* (Autobiography)

READING FOCUS

1. Active readers interact with what they read, responding to the work's ideas.
2. Analyze the story or stories each writer is trying to tell. It helps you understand what you've read.
3. Look at a piece of literature from several angles and think about "what if" situations that might change how you perceive a text.
4. Active reading requires close attention to the choice of words and the way they are arranged.
5. Knowing about a writer's life can help you better understand his or her work.

WRITING FOCUS

1. Summarize your understanding of a poem and describe your responses to it.
2. Make a story chart for a poem connecting it to incidents in your life.
3. Write an interpretation of a poem, considering all of the various perspectives you explored.
4. Explore the poet's style and language, focusing on the title and arrangement of a poem.
5. Examine poetry for autobiographical details and compare how the details are presented.

One Interactions with the Text

Critical Reading

FOCUS

Umberto Eco, on reading: "Every text is a lazy machine asking the reader to do some of its work."

Critical readers know that taking notes as they read can help them focus on various literary elements of a work.

BACKGROUND

Lesson One, "Interactions with the Text," is designed to show students how and why careful readers mark a text as they read. Have students examine the poem "Early in the Morning" to see what an annotated poem looks like. Point out to students that what they have before them is not the only way to annotate this poem but rather one particular reader's thoughtful markings. The annotations should help draw their attention to the poem's meaning. Ask them to notice how section I is a description of the narrator's mother's morning routine. Section II is a commentary on the significance of these actions based upon what the narrator, now an adult, knows about the intimacy of marriage.

➤ On their first reading of the poem "The Gift," students should take note of the poem's action. A little boy gets a splinter; his father pulls it out. A woman gets a splinter; her husband pulls it out. Students may begin to wonder if the boy and the husband are the same person. On a second reading, students can concentrate on interpreting the author's underlying meaning. The gift that Lee refers to in the title is both the story the father tells and love. The father gives it to the son who in turn is able to give it to his wife. The splinter is Lee's way of symbolizing the obstacles to love and happiness that all humans face. Because of his father's gift, the speaker does not need to "lift up my wound and cry." Thanks to his father's gift of love, he is able to bestow his own symbol of love—a kiss.

FOR DISCUSSION AND REFLECTION

Ask students to reflect on how annotating a text helps them to understand what they are reading. (Annotation makes reading a more active process. Often, inexperienced readers do not realize that texts are, in Umberto Eco's words, lazy machines that expect the reader to do some of the work.)

Writing

QUICK ASSESS

Do students' paragraphs:

✓ reflect an understanding of the poem's underlying meaning?

✓ include an explanation or discussion of the poem's language?

Students are asked to write a brief summary of "The Gift" and then explain their reactions to the poem. As a prewriting activity, have them revisit their annotations of the poem.

READING AND WRITING EXTENSIONS

➤ Ask students to compare and contrast "Early in the Morning" with "The Gift." What features of the poems help them to know these were written by the same person?

➤ As an additional challenge, have students apply what they have learned about annotation to another text: a poem, a copy of the first paragraph of a novel, a copy of a page from their social studies textbook.

➤ Have students reread "Early in the Morning" and write a poem describing the early-morning routine of someone in their household. It could be the student's own routine.

Two Story Connections

Critical Reading

FOCUS

Another angle of literacy has to do with the ways readers connect with a piece of writing. As we read, we connect with the plot, tone, writer's intent, and underlying message of a work.

BACKGROUND

One way to connect to a text is to relate to the story being told. (Keep in mind that nonfiction and poetry can tell a story, just as a novel or play tells a story.) Even more specifically, readers connect with the conflict(s) or problem(s) or incident(s) described in a work. They think about how they might feel in a given situation and then compare their reactions to the characters' reactions. For example, who in their lives has given them a gift of love? Was their reaction similar to the boy's reaction in "The Gift"?

➤ Readers can also connect with the characters, speaker, narrator, and author of a work. For example, which people or events described in "The Gift" does the reader find most interesting? Which people or event in the poem is the reader likely to ignore? What does the reader think about Lee's writing style?

➤ A reader will also connect to the underlying meaning or message of a text. How does the event described relate to my own life? How do my personal feelings or opinions affect my opinion of the writing?

➤ Another way to connect to a text is to evaluate it. Was this a worthwhile piece to read? What is it about "The Gift" that does or does not appeal to me? Is "The Gift" a more engaging poem than "Eating Together"? Why or why not?

FOR DISCUSSION AND REFLECTION

Discuss with students why it is important for a reader to connect with a text.

➤ What sort of connections do you generally make to a text? Describe them. (Answers will vary, but should focus on how an event or detail in a story reminds students of something in their lives.)

➤ What writing do students find it difficult to connect with? Why? (Answers will vary.)

Writing

QUICK ASSESS
Are students' charts:
✓ complete?
✓ thoughtfully done?
✓ easily understood?

Students are asked to make story charts for "The Gift." On their charts they'll make notes about the different "incidents" that Lee describes and the ways in which they connected to the poem.

READING AND WRITING EXTENSIONS

➤ As an additional challenge, have students take an item from the "Similar incidents I know of" column of their charts and write a poem or short story in which they explore the incident. Remind them how important it is for their readers to be able to connect with the story they want to tell.

➤ Invite students to thumb through a volume of poetry and find a poem they like. Ask them to do a dramatic reading of the poem for the class. After reading the poem, they can explain how they connected to it.

Three Shifting Perspectives

Critical Reading

FOCUS

Analyzing why a writer chose a certain point of view or perspective is a key part of understanding the author's intentions and feelings.

BACKGROUND

Critical readers know that an important part of understanding a work is being able to make inferences about the different perspectives associated with a piece of writing. These perspectives include those of the author, the narrator, the characters, and the speaker (in a poem). In addition to these perspectives, critical readers know that they bring their own perspectives to a piece of writing. How do the readers' experiences, opinions, and attitudes affect their perceptions of the text?

➤ One technique for examining perspective is to ask "What if" questions. Asking these questions can help a reader uncover the underlying meaning of a text. Consider Li-Young Lee's perspective in "Eating Together." The poem tells a simple story of a family sitting down to dinner. He describes the mother and her lovingly prepared meal. As he considers the meal, Lee is reminded of his father, who "lay down / to sleep like a snow-covered road. . . ." Instead of being a poem of mourning, however, "Eating Together" is more of a celebration of the simple pleasures in life.

➤ Lee's use of figurative language and poetic devices help him reveal his loving perspective toward his family. For example, the alliteration—his repetition of the *s* sound, for example—creates a peaceful, soothing mood for the poem. This peaceful mood helps the reader understand Lee's attitude toward his father's death.

FOR DISCUSSION AND REFLECTION

Ask students to discuss the shifting perspectives in Lee's poem "Eating Together."

➤ What is the mood of this poem? (peaceful, elegiac, and simply celebratory)

➤ Is there a point in the poem when the mood changes? (Yes, in the eighth line, when the poet remembers his father and moves from a description of the meal to an elegy for his father's death.)

➤ Consider the last line of the poem. Does Lee end on a depressing note or an optimistic note? Explain. (The last line is describing his father's death, but it is optimistic about what the death means.)

Writing

QUICK ASSESS

Do students:

✔ show they grasp the meaning of the poem?

✔ discuss the poem in terms of perspective?

✔ demonstrate an ability to consider poetic elements?

Students are asked to write an interpretation of Lee's poem, analyzing the various perspectives available in the text.

READING AND WRITING EXTENSIONS

➤ What images come to mind when students read "Eating Together"? Ask students to draw a picture of the thing they visualize. Then have them write a one-paragraph explanation of the image—and their art.

➤ Invite students to choose one symbol from the poem to analyze in a short essay. For example, they might choose to explore the trout, "seasoned with slivers of ginger . . ." or the father, who "lay down /to sleep like a snow-covered road. . . ." Students should explain what the symbol means and then also discuss the effect the symbol has on the rest of the poem.

Four Language and Craft

Critical Reading

FOCUS

Writers make deliberate word choices when writing, just as writers make deliberate choices about their structure and style. A reader needs to be able to interpret the reasons for those choices and then be able to reflect on how they affect the meaning of a text.

BACKGROUND

Another important angle of literacy is the ability to understand the author's language and craft. A reader's first step in understanding language is to note words that are unfamiliar or confusing. After that, the reader can begin thinking about the connotations (the emotional associations surrounding a word) and denotations (the strict dictionary definition of a word) of words that seem particularly important or significant. For example, a word that is repeated often in a piece of writing would probably be considered important. A word that is used as a part of a metaphor, or a word that is used as a symbol, might also be considered important.

➤ Another job for the reader is to understand the author's craft—the style and structure of a piece. A reader needs to pause and consider how the piece is put together. What are the sentences or lines like? What do you notice about individual paragraphs or stanzas?

➤ In Lesson Four, students will explore Li-Young Lee's language, structure, and style in "Mnemonic." In this poem, Lee explains how an old blue sweater his father once owned serves as a reminder of all that he loved about his father. Before they begin reading, ask students to define and discuss the word "mnemonic." What mnemonics do students use in their own lives?

FOR DISCUSSION AND REFLECTION

Discuss with students Lee's writing style in "Mnemonic."

➤ Which words or phrases caught your attention when you read the poem for the first time? (Responses will vary.)

➤ Does Lee use symbolism in "Mnemonic"? Does he use metaphors? Explain. (The entire poem is about a symbol: the blue sweater. It is a symbol of Lee's father and their relationship. The only metaphor in the poem is "memory, a heap of details. . .")

Writing

QUICK ASSESS

Do students:

✓ attempt to imitate Lee's style?

✓ include the whole of the original story?

✓ make careful and deliberate word choices?

Students are asked to consider other titles for Lee's poem. As a prewriting activity, they'll think about the structure and style of Lee's poem and note their observations on a chart.

READING AND WRITING EXTENSIONS

➤ As an additional challenge, ask students to do a language analysis of one stanza from "Mnemonic." In their analyses, students should explore individual word choices in addition to Lee's use of imagery and figurative language.

➤ Have students check the library or their literature anthologies for a short story they might analyze in terms of language and craft. Have them begin by writing a brief plot summary. Then they can take a paragraph or two to explain the author's style, language, structure, and viewpoint, comparing it with Lee's.

Five Focus on the Writer

Critical Reading

FOCUS

Sometimes discovering information about an author's background can help a reader see an author's work in a different light, or help a reader get a handle on a work that is difficult to understand.

BACKGROUND

In this lesson, students will read a short excerpt from Li-Young Lee's autobiography. Afterward they will be invited to reread the poems used in the previous four lessons. As they read, students will search for details about Lee's life. These details may help students gain new insights into the poetry. During their rereadings, students might note, for example:

➤ Li-Young Lee wrote in another part of *The Winged Seed*: "As I was growing up in my father's house, it seemed to me that his entire life was divided between composing sermons and praying for or ministering to the bodies and souls of the members of that church situated on a hill. . . ." Lee's father was obviously a dynamic presence in his family and in his community. His mother seems like the gentle nurturer of the family. Both parents are clearly important to Li-Young, which is perhaps why he seems to focus so much of his writing on one or the other. (See "Early in the Morning," "The Gift," "Eating Together," and "Mnemonic.")

FOR DISCUSSION AND REFLECTION

Discuss with students how their attitudes toward Lee's poetry have changed now that they know something about the poet's life.

➤ What elements of his own life does Lee incorporate into his poetry? (Lee incorporates many events from his childhood and family life.)

➤ Do students find Lee's poetry more or less interesting now that they know a little of his background? (Responses will vary.)

Writing

QUICK ASSESS

Do students' charts:

✓ include information about all three poems?

✓ include direct comparisons to the poems?

Students are invited to create charts that help them explore the autobiographical elements of Lee's poetry. As a part of this exercise they are asked to examine "The Gift," "Eating Together," and "Mnemonic."

READING AND WRITING EXTENSION

➤ Ask students to compare the writing style Lee uses in his autobiography to the writing style he uses in his poetry. What are some similarities and differences? Students might explore one or more of these topics in their comparisons:

- Lee's use of figurative language
- Lee's use of imagery
- Lee's use of formal versus informal language

Unit Overview

In this unit, students will study the collaboration between readers and authors that is such an important part of the reading process. By reading and responding to a variety of texts, they will explore various aspects of this collaboration, including stepping into a text; the many ways our experiences affect our interpretations of a piece of literature; and the way we make predictions during reading.

LITERATURE FOCUS

Lesson	*Literature*
1. You, as Reader	**Bel Kaufman**, "Sunday in the Park" (Story)
2. Reading Experiences	
3. What's Next?	**Salazar Arrué**, "We Bad" (Short Story)
4. Other Worlds	**Chinua Achebe**, "Why Tortoise's Shell Is Not Smooth" (Short Story)
5. Beginnings, Beginnings	**Stephen Dunn**, from "Gambling: Remembrance and Assertions" (Nonfiction)
	Michael Ondaatje, from "The War Between Men and Women" (Short Story)
	Tibor Déry, from "The Circus" (Short Story)

READING FOCUS

1. Readers enter the imaginative world created by authors and locate themselves in the story.

2. Your memories and experiences influence the way you read. Because of that a story can sometimes have a different meaning for every reader.

3. As you read, stop to predict what might happen next. Take time to think about what characters will do or what events might take place.

4. Sometimes writers stretch our minds as readers by taking us to far-off worlds built in their imaginations.

5. Authors try to hook readers with the beginnings of their stories. Strong beginnings create interest and get readers involved with a story.

WRITING FOCUS

1. Write pieces of advice about the best ways for a reader to engage with a text.

2. Write about a personal experience that connects to the story and then write about another work to which you had a strong personal response.

3. Make predictions about a story and write an ending based on these predictions.

4. Fill out a fantasy and realism chart, analyzing how realistic details contribute to fantastical stories.

5. Evaluate various story openings and their effectiveness as hooks.

One You, as Reader

Critical Reading

FOCUS

This lesson is designed to help students understand the collaboration between the author and the reader. Authors expect readers to "suspend their disbelief" and step into the imaginary worlds they describe. Readers expect writers to provide them with plenty of detail so that it is easy for them to become involved in the story.

BACKGROUND

Bel Kaufman on writing fiction " . . . Fictional characters take readers on a voyage of exploration that leads to surprising truths."

➤ Bel Kaufman's short story "Sunday in the Park" is engaging from the very first paragraph. Because the situation described in this story is so universal—a bully on a playground—students should have no trouble stepping into Kaufman's imaginary world.

➤ In the first paragraph of the story, Kaufman describes an afternoon at the park that one mother finds close to perfect: "*How good this is*, she thought, and almost smiled at her sense of well-being." As soon as the first fistful of sand is thrown, the reader is hooked. Now fully engaged with the text, the reader can sit one park bench over from Morton and his wife and watch the fight as it develops. Kaufman's ambiguous, even abrupt, ending leaves the reader wondering: "What just happened here?"

➤ The ambiguity of Kaufman's ending is an invitation to readers to relate to the story in terms of their own experiences—or in terms of their own personalities. Would they also have spoken to Morton in a voice "thin and cold and penetrating with contempt" or would they have sympathized with Morton's irritation with Larry?

FOR DISCUSSION AND REFLECTION

Discuss with students why it is so vital that a reader engage with the story.

➤ What techniques can a writer use to help readers step into the setting and action? (Possible responses: concrete description, vivid details, a strong hook, dialogue, etc.)

➤ Do we step into nonfiction or poetry in the same ways we step into fiction? Explain. (Answers will vary, but should focus on the different intentions of poets, fiction writers, and nonfiction writers.)

Writing

QUICK ASSESS

Does the statement of advice:

✔ show how elements of setting, style, and character can affect a reader's ability to become involved in a story?

In pairs, students will discuss the various ways a reader can engage with a story and then write statements of advice on how to "get into" a story.

READING AND WRITING EXTENSIONS

➤ As an additional challenge, students might write a continuation of the sidewalk conversation between Larry's parents. Students' dialogues could begin at the point where the mother says, "'You and who else?'" When they've finished, students can discuss whether their continuations enhance or detract from Kaufman's story.

➤ Have students read a piece of nonfiction to see if the techniques they use for engaging with fiction also apply to a work of nonfiction. Students can explain their findings in a brief analytical essay.

Two Reading Experiences

Critical Reading

FOCUS

Your experience influences the way you intepret and feel about what you read.

BACKGROUND

"Reading Experiences" examines the ways readers' own experiences affect their understanding of a piece of literature. Students are asked to reflect on "Sunday in the Park" and then decide what in the story reminds them of their own lives.

➤ One of the reasons Kaufman's story appeals to readers is because it feels so familiar. When the little boy throws sand at Larry, the reader feels a sense of literary *déjà vu:* "That happened to me once, or that *reminds me* of something that happened to me once."

➤ After the sand-throwing incident, Morton must decide whether or not he should fight the bully's father. At this point in the story, the reader is inclined to step in and take sides. Should Morton back down, or should he fight? Should Morton's wife support his decision or criticize it? The reader can't help but think about what he or she might do in a similar situation.

FOR DISCUSSION AND REFLECTION

Ask students to work in pairs to discuss how their own experiences affect their readings of "Sunday in the Park." The partners might also consider these questions:

➤ Would an adult have a difficult time relating to this story? Explain why or why not. (No, as it is told from the perspective of the mother.)

➤ What are some techniques authors use to make their stories seem familiar? Why are these techniques important? (Possible responses: the commonplace details, which evoke the mood and place; the dialogue, which seems directly from ordinary life; the strong emotions, which everyone has felt.)

Writing

QUICK ASSESS
Do students' paragraphs:

✔ explain why the work affected them so?

✔ compare the work to their own lives?

Students are asked to think of a work they had a strong reaction to and then write a paragraph explaining what in their own lives caused them to react this way.

READING AND WRITING EXTENSIONS

➤ Ask students to write a book review in which they describe a book or poem that had a profound effect on them.

➤ Have the class vote on the types of books that are most popular with high school students. What kinds of books do they relate to best? Ask students to explain their votes.

Three What's Next?

Critical Reading

FOCUS

Encourage students to make predictions as they read. Making predictions helps maintain—and sometimes heightens—a reader's interest in a text.

BACKGROUND

The short story "We Bad" is a good example of a text that invites predictions. Its narrative is more roundabout than straightforward, and its characters are more ambiguous than transparent. Salazar Arrué clearly has written this story with an eye to keeping the reader guessing.

➤ Throughout the story, Arrué uses foreshadowing to heighten the reader's anticipation and encourage us to make predictions about what will happen next. When we read about the boy's fear of snakes, for example, we wonder if he will be bitten. When we see the travelers discomfort after the first day, we wonder how they can possibly survive the long journey.

➤ In addition to using foreshadowing, Arrué sets up several narrative traps that force readers to stop, assess, and predict. One such trap is set when Arrué abruptly moves us to the bandits' camp. As soon as we understand where we are, we begin to make guesses about what the bandits might do. Later Arrué shows us that we would have been better served by making predictions about what the bandits had already done.

FOR DISCUSSION AND REFLECTION

Ask students to work together in small groups to discuss the predictions they made while reading "We Bad."

➤ What effect did students' predictions have on their interest in the story? (Responses will vary.)

➤ What other types of writing encourage readers to make predictions? Do we, for example, make predictions as we read newspaper articles? Do we make predictions as we read poetry? (Responses will vary, but should arrive at the conclusion that making predictions is valuable in all reading.)

Writing

QUICK ASSESS

Do students:

✔ explain their reactions to the end of the story?

✔ compare the outcome to their predictions?

✔ summarize why making predictions is an important part of active reading?

Students are asked to write an ending for the story using clues given by the author and their own predictions about what might happen. As a prediscussion activity, students will review the predictions they made in the middle of the story so that they can compare their predictions with those of the other students.

READING AND WRITING EXTENSIONS

➤ Ask students to reread "We Bad." How are their reactions to the story different now that they know what happened in the end? Do they enjoy the story less or more? Ask them to explain their reactions in a paragraph.

➤ As an additional challenge, have students share with the class a work of nonfiction that they think encourages readers to make predictions.

Four Other Worlds

Critical Reading

FOCUS

Chinua Achebe, on writing: "The writer's duty is not to beat this morning's headlines in topicality; it is to explore the depth of human characters."

This lesson explores the ways writers present fantasy worlds to readers.

BACKGROUND

Chinua Achebe's fable is an interesting combination of reality and fantasy that keeps the reader guessing right up to the end. Students learn that although the worlds may be imaginary, the author must include some elements of realism in order to maintain the reader's interest.

➤ Notice the juxtaposition of realism and fantasy in Achebe's story. A tortoise that speaks, reasons, and flies (fantasy) is described by a mother to her daughter who listens attentively and occasionally interrupts with questions (realism).

➤ Fantasy and reality coexist in other aspects of Achebe's story. For example, although the birds have human qualities, they also act like birds: they fly in a flock, they "peck" at their food, and they give the impression that they are squawking, especially when they're complaining.

FOR DISCUSSION AND REFLECTION

Discuss with students the details in "Why Tortoise's Shell Is Not Smooth" that helped them feel a part of the world described.

➤ Why are a few realistic details important to a fantasy story? (They give the reader a foothold for imagining the world in their own head.)

➤ What part of the story did students find most interesting or entertaining? Ask them to explain why. (Responses will vary.)

Writing

QUICK ASSESS

Do students' charts:

✓ reflect an understanding of Achebe's fable?

✓ correctly categorize realistic and fantastic elements?

✓ reflect an ability to make inferences about character and plot?

After they've finished reading, students are asked to work on a chart that categorizes fantastic and realistic elements in Achebe's fable. Students' charts should be as detailed as possible. You should encourage them to use quotations from the text when appropriate.

READING AND WRITING EXTENSIONS

➤ Have students think of a TV show they've seen that combines realistic and fantastic elements. Ask them to write a paragraph describing the show.

➤ As an additional challenge, have students make a story map for a fable they'd like to write. Their maps should include descriptions of the various realistic and fantastic elements they'd want to include in their fables.

➤ Ask students to work together to make a Fable, Folklore, and Fantasy reading list for a particular age group. Students should be prepared to describe each title they included on the reading list.

Five Beginnings, Beginnings

Critical Reading

FOCUS

The opening paragraph, or hook, in a story is immensely important in setting the scene and catching the attention of the reader.

BACKGROUND

This lesson explores the various ways an author can use the opening paragraph of a work to command the attention of the reader. Students are asked to review the first few paragraphs of the three stories they read in this unit ("Sunday in the Park," "We Bad," and "Why Tortoise's Shell Is Not Smooth"), and then judge the effect of each story's opening.

➤ Bel Kaufman uses the technique of *scene setting* as her "hook." Her description of a "perfect" day in the park is an invitation to the reader to start thinking about what might go wrong. We continue reading because we want to find out what happens.

➤ Achebe lets the reader know right from the start that the mother has a story worth telling and expects us—his readers—to pull up a mat and listen along with Ezinma.

➤ Salazar Arrué uses *dialogue* as a means of hooking the reader. The opening exchange between Goyo and the boy is so strange that we feel compelled to read on and find out what exactly they're doing.

FOR DISCUSSION AND REFLECTION

Discuss with students why the first few paragraphs of a work are so vital.

➤ What elements should readers look for in a story's opening? (They should look for clues about the mood and tone of a story, the main characters, the main conflict, or the setting.)

➤ Which techniques for story openers are most effective? Why? (Answers will vary, but will reflect the need for gripping descriptions of characters, settings, etc., at the start.)

➤ Have students consider the various ways writers grab our attention in other literary genres, such as the mystery novel or newspaper article.

Writing

QUICK ASSESS

Does each student:

✓ identify the technique (hook, character throwing, dialogue, etc.) used?

✓ assess the effectiveness of the opening and offer support for the assessment?

Students are asked to fill out a chart evaluating the effectiveness of the hooks from the literature in the previous lessons. They are also asked to read different story openings and then decide what type of story will follow from the hook.

READING AND WRITING EXTENSIONS

➤ Have students look through a literature anthology or collection of short stories to find examples of effective story openers. Later they can explain why they feel the beginnings are effective.

➤ *Dark and Stormy Rides Again* (1996) is a collection of opening sentences for bad imaginary novels. It is part of a series of books from the Bulwer-Lytton Fiction Contest. Read students some of the openers from this collection and then have them create their own entries.

➤ Ask students to think of a story they've read that they didn't like for one reason or another. How did the story's opening affect their judgment? Have them write a paragraph that explains their views.

Unit Overview

In "The Stories We Tell," students will explore what makes an author's writing memorable. What can an author do to ensure that his or her story will appeal to a vast number of people? How does an author know that he or she is describing an experience that others will be able to connect to? To help them explore the world of storytelling—and what writers have to offer readers—students will read and respond to excerpts from three well-known authors: Isabel Allende, Jamaica Kincaid, and Zora Neale Hurston.

LITERATURE FOCUS

Lesson	*Literature*
1. When the Subject Is "I"	**Isabel Allende**, from *Paula* (Nonfiction)
2. Story Descriptions	
3. Events in Stories	**Jamaica Kincaid**, from *Annie John* (Novel)
4. Story and Its Messages	**Zora Neale Hurston**, "I Get Born" from *Dust Tracks on the Road* (Autobiography)
5. On With the Story	**Natalie Goldberg**, from *Long, Quiet Highway* (Nonfiction)

READING FOCUS

1. Memories—and telling about them in rich detail—are what make personal narratives interesting and powerful.

2. Sensory descriptions not only help readers locate themselves in the story, but also intensify the meaning of the story.

3. Plots in stories generally follow a three-part structure. The beginning introduces a conflict or problem. The middle describes a series of complications in the attempt to solve the problem. The end generally provides a resolution.

4. Writers choose to relate certain events because of what they "tell." Watch for the message behind authors' choices of subjects.

5. Choosing a topic is the first step in writing a story. But how that story gets told is what creates a memorable and participatory experience for the reader.

WRITING FOCUS

1. Create a memory catalog that lists events from your life, which would be good subjects to write about.

2. Make a sensory description chart and analyze how sensory descriptions affect the reader.

3. Use a plot line to examine how a plot is structured and where the tension is greatest.

4. Write a short piece, analyzing Hurston's message in the excerpt from her autobiography.

5. Draft a personal narrative, shaping it around the three-part plot structure.

One When the Subject Is "I"

C r i t i c a l   R e a d i n g

FOCUS

Isabel Allende wrote "Listen, Paula. I am going to tell you a story so that when you wake up you will not feel so lost."

BACKGROUND

This lesson invites students to examine what makes for effective personal narratives. As an example of an effective personal narrative, students will read an excerpt from *Paula*, Isabel Allende's moving account of her life as a devoted daughter and a loving mother.

➤ *Paula* is a memoir that binds past and present. It is first and foremost an account of the year Allende spent caring for her critically ill daughter, Paula. As a sort of gift for Paula, Allende begins to tell the story of her life. In her narrative, Allende switches from present to past to present again—interrupting her story to bring Paula a glass of water, for example, or put a cool compress on her head. "I place one hand over my heart, close my eyes, and concentrate" is one of Allende's many signals that she will leave the present for a moment or two in order to reveal an anecdote about her youth.

➤ In this excerpt from *Paula*, Allende reveals the traumatic effect her mother's illness had on her when she was a child. Notice Allende's success at maintaining a single point of view in her story. Because she tells the story through the eyes of a seven-year-old child, she can comment only on the things that a child is likely notice: the rain puddles that are worth jumping, the poplar tree that is a scrawny sentinel, the heavy-framed mirror which must be avoided in case the Devil is lingering in its image. This limits our view of the story while at the same time generates interest in and sympathy for the author as a child.

FOR DISCUSSION AND REFLECTION

Discuss with students the various ways a writer can make a personal narrative interesting and memorable.

➤ How does a writer's style affect our interest in a story? (The writer's style creates the tone and, hence, how we react to the story.)

➤ What reasons might an author have for writing a personal narrative? (Some possible responses: to document an important event or time period, to sort out feelings about a specific subject, to entertain, to justify an action or idea, etc.)

W r i t i n g

QUICK ASSESS

Do students' memory catalogs:

✔ reflect the whole span of their lives?

✔ include at least two categories of their own invention?

Students are asked to create memory catalogs of their own experiences. Encourage students to be as detailed as possible in their catalogs.

READING AND WRITING EXTENSIONS

➤ Ask students to write a paragraph that explores one topic from their memory catalog. Their paragraphs should be written from the first-person point of view and follow the format of a personal narrative. If they like, they might use the Allende excerpt as a model for their writing style.

➤ Have students think about other autobiographies they've read. Which would they consider most powerful? Why?

TWO Story Descriptions

Critical Reading

FOCUS

Isabel Allende, on using memories to create a personal narrative:

"I take one step backward, another, and with each step decades are erased…."

BACKGROUND

In this lesson, students examine how an author's descriptions contribute to the overall mood or tone of the story. Students are invited to return to the Allende excerpt and read it again, this time keeping an eye out for Allende's use of sensory details.

➤ Notice how Allende gives equal weight to all five senses when she writes. Because she places so much emphasis on the senses, Allende comes close to convincing her readers to take a bite of the buttered bread, or plug their noses to block the odor of onions. We feel young Isabel's revulsion at the sight of the "walls of the cavernous kitchen which are spotted with grease." By describing what she sees, hears, touches, and even smells on this difficult day, Allende brings a vividness to her writing that allows the reader to step into the scene and feel a part of the action.

➤ Notice also how Allende's skillful use of sensory description helps set the mood for the story. The "fly-specked lightbulbs" and the echo of Isabel's reluctant footsteps on the stairs create an atmosphere of gloom that matches exactly the gloom—and dread—that young Isabel must have felt.

FOR DISCUSSION AND REFLECTION

Discuss with students why sensory details help intensify the meaning of the story.

➤ How do sensory details contribute to a piece of writing? (Sensory details help establish the tone and mood of a piece of writing and help the reader focus on the theme or main idea of the work.)

➤ What other kinds of writing—besides personal narratives—require the use of sensory details? Explain. (All writing benefits from details, as they draw the reader into the world of the text.)

Writing

QUICK ASSESS
Do students' charts:

✓ reflect an understanding of the different types of sensory descriptions?

✓ show careful analysis of Allende's use of sensory detail?

Students are asked to select one type of sensory description (sight, smell, taste, etc.) and trace it through the Allende excerpt. They will then complete a sensory description chart that will help them analyze the effect description has on meaning.

READING AND WRITING EXTENSIONS

➤ As an additional challenge, have students continue their work on the sensory description chart by tracing the ways Allende uses the other four senses.

➤ Sensory description is equally important in poetry. Ask students to find and share a poem that is filled with sensory detail. Have the student read the poem aloud to the class.

Three Events in Stories

Critical Reading

FOCUS

The traditional dramatic structure of stories—used in novels, plays, films, television, etc.—is a three-part structure: presentation of a conflict, attempted solutions, and eventual resolution.

BACKGROUND

Lesson Three, "Events in Stories," is a discussion of plot and the various ways an author moves the action forward in a story. Students learn that although every story has a plot, some plots are more skillfully done than others. This excerpt from Jamaica Kincaid's *Annie John* provides an example of a well-constructed plot.

➤ Most plots have a three-part structure: conflict, complication, and resolution. The mother and daughter's argument about the marbles forms the basis of the plot's conflict. As the story moves on, the argument between the two characters becomes increasingly more heated (rising tension). Kincaid inserts complications when she has the mother tell the story of the snake.

➤ Notice how the plot shifts when the mother tells about the incident with the snake. Suddenly the reader is privy to the mother's point of view, and we begin to think that maybe Annie *should* give up her marbles. Ultimately there is resolution to the conflict when Annie decides to keep quiet.

FOR DISCUSSION AND REFLECTION

Discuss with students the three parts of a plot's structure.

➤ Why is it so important that a plot have a conflict? (Conflicts give shape to a plot and create the dramatic structure which compel a reader to read on.

➤ How do you think Kincaid's story would have been different without the complication of the mother's anecdote? (Responses will vary, but should focus on how the mother's anecdote provides a different perspective on the conflict between mother and daughter.)

➤ What is the effect of a plot with no resolution? What is the effect of a plot that is resolved too easily? Explain. (A plot with no resolution is maddening because it feels unfinished to the reader. A plot too-easily resolved lacks the tension that keeps readers interested in a story.)

Writing

QUICK ASSESS

Do students' plot summaries:

✔ reflect the correct sequence of events in the story?

✔ demonstrate an understanding of the three elements of plot?

Students are asked to make a plot line of Kincaid's story and then explain in three sentences the plot of the excerpt from *Annie John*.

READING AND WRITING EXTENSIONS

➤ Have students write a new ending to the story of the marbles. How would they resolve the conflict between mother and daughter?

➤ Invite students to find and share a newspaper or magazine story that reminds them of the conflict-complications-resolution described in the excerpt from *Annie John*.

Four Story and Its Messages

Critical Reading

FOCUS

Finding the main idea is an essential part of understanding what you read. The main idea is the point or message the author is trying to get across.

BACKGROUND

"Story and Its Messages" examines the various ways writers send messages to their readers. In some cases, a writer will state the message or main idea explicitly. In other cases, a reader will have to *infer* the message or main idea from what the author has to say about the subject. Zora Neale Hurston's piece "I Get Born" has both a stated and an implied message.

➤ In this anecdote, Hurston uses the story of her birth as a means of revealing her views on human nature. An explicit statement of her message can be found at the end of the piece: "There is nothing to make you like other human beings so much as doing things for them."

➤ In addition to offering an explicit message about her views on human nature, Hurston encourages her readers to infer what they can from her story. By emphasizing the white man's role in her birth, Hurston shows the reader that it's possible to be humane in our dealings with others.

FOR DISCUSSION AND REFLECTION

Discuss with students the various ways of interpreting an author's main idea or message.

➤ Why is it important for a reader to try to understand the author's main idea? (Finding the main idea allows you to understand why the author wrote the piece and what the author is trying to say.)

➤ Why might an author choose to imply a message rather than state it directly? (Possible response: an outright statement of message would bog down the plot structure of a story or personal narrative.)

Writing

QUICK ASSESS

Does the student's piece:

✔ include a thoughtful discussion of Hurston's message?

✔ show an understanding of the differences between explicit and implied messages?

Students are asked to write a short reflective piece about the message(s) they found in Hurston's anecdote. As a prewriting activity, have students work together in small groups to answer the questions at the top of page 48.

READING AND WRITING EXTENSIONS

➤ Ask students to write their own version of "I Get Born." What message do they have for their readers?

➤ Have students think about another autobiographical piece they've read. How does this other piece of writing differ from Hurston's anecdote? Have students write a paragraph in which they compare and contrast the two pieces in terms of style, tone, and message.

Five On With the Story

Critical Reading

FOCUS

Natalie Goldberg wrote "Almost any topic was okay, because once you began, you entered your own mind and your mind had its own paths to travel."

BACKGROUND

"On With the Story" helps students tie together what they've learned about telling stories. Before they begin the activities in this lesson, you might have students review the other four lessons in the unit. Asking students questions similar to the ones below will help them focus on what they've learned.

➤ How does an author choose a topic?

➤ What are some techniques an author can use to make the topic interesting to readers?

➤ What are the characteristics of first-person point of view?

➤ What makes for an effective personal narrative? What can detract from the effectiveness of a personal narrative?

➤ What is sensory description?

➤ Why do authors use sensory description in their writing?

➤ What makes for a good plot?

➤ Why is a story's underlying message important?

FOR DISCUSSION AND REFLECTION

Discuss with students various techniques for maintaining a reader's interest.

➤ What effect does writing style have on a reader's interest? (Responses will vary.)

➤ How much description is too much description? How do you know? (Responses will vary.)

➤ What does it mean to "know your audience"? (It means an author must use details, language, and ideas that are accessible and interesting to his or her readers.)

Writing

QUICK ASSESS

Do students' narratives:

✓ recall a memory or event from the first-person point of view?

✓ remain focused on one memory or event?

✓ appear well organized and well thought out?

Students are asked to write a draft of a personal narrative. As a prewriting activity, students should look over the memory catalogs they made for an earlier lesson and see if they can find a topic for their narratives.

READING AND WRITING EXTENSIONS

➤ Have students reread the Natalie Goldberg quote on page 49 of their books. What do they think of Goldberg's ideas for things that she might write about? Invite them to write an essay using one of Goldberg's topics: "apples in August, shoes, my grandmother's feet, stairs I climbed."

➤ Ask students to thumb through some literature anthologies to find another example of a personal narrative they find interesting. Ask them to read the story and then report to the class.

➤ Invite students to write an essay in which they compare the characteristics of an autobiography to the characteristics of a biography. How do the two genres differ? How are they similar?

Unit Overview

In "Framing and Focusing," students will explore how an author's use of detail and description affects a reader's ability to form a picture of the action. Why does a writer want a reader to be able to see the scene? How can we hear the author's descriptions? To explore how perspectives on a story are formed—and how individual perspectives can shift—students will read and respond to two poems, a newspaper article, and an excerpt from an autobiography.

LITERATURE FOCUS

Lesson	Literature
1. Perceiving	**Mary TallMountain**, "The Last Wolf" (Poetry)
2. Noticing Details	**Ernie Pyle**, from *Brave Men* (Nonfiction)
3. Framing the Scene	
4. Listening to the Text	**Gary Paulsen**, from *Woodsong* (Autobiography)
5. Making Mental Movies	**Quincy Troupe**, "A Poem for 'Magic' " (Poetry)

READING FOCUS

1. Think about the first impression a piece of writing makes. Then shape or fine-tune your impression as you read.
2. Noticing detail is essential to getting an impression of a scene.
3. Concentrate on the pictures writers create through the arrangements of details in their descriptions.
4. Adding sound effects and dialogue as you read helps you fully visualize a scene.
5. Notice the ways writers play with words and images to convey both sight and sound.

WRITING FOCUS

1. Write about your impressions of a poem and how they evolved.
2. Create a double-entry log: a listing of details and the impressions you drew from them.
3. Draw a picture of the scene, focusing on the details included.
4. Create storyboards for a scene, including dialogue, sound effects, and the images you want to film.
5. Create a list of words that describe a performer and then use these words to write a poem.

One Perceiving

Critical Reading

FOCUS

When reading or listening, our brains form an immediate impression about what we see or hear. This impression is the basis for our understanding of a piece; through rereading, drawing, discussion, etc., we refine it to create a full picture of what we read.

BACKGROUND

In this first lesson students will concentrate on understanding how an author's use of detail affects a reader's first impression. Students will begin their study of details by reading Mary TallMountain's poem "The Last Wolf"—which creates a strong first impression.

➤ In "The Last Wolf" TallMountain explores two distinct yet related themes: the reverence for nature and animals and the idea of "progress" and the toll it takes on human life. Both of TallMountain's themes are readily apparent to the reader because of the poet's language and imagery.

➤ The very first image the reader sees in this poem is the wolf. We "frame and focus" the image of this magnificent animal and its frantic run through a busy city. Because of TallMountain's use of sensory language, we are almost able to hear his "baying" cries, his "low whine," and his "snuffle" at the door.

➤ Another image that stands out from the very first reading is that of the person who waits alone to greet the wolf. We can "see" the bed she sits upon; we come close to sharing her urge to reach out and touch the wolf's muzzle. The speaker's lament comes through loudly and clearly. At the end of the poem, we understand her grief and despair as she says, "I know what they have done."

FOR DISCUSSION AND REFLECTION

Discuss with students why first impressions are so important to a reader.

➤ What techniques can a writer use to help create a strong first impression? (Possible answers include vivid details, a strong hook or opening, sentence structure, etc.)

➤ What effect does an author's style have on a reader's first impression? (The most important elements of an author's style—structure, word choice, and tone—also create the reader's first impression.)

Writing

QUICK ASSESS

Do students:

✓ clearly explain their reactions to TallMountain's poem?

✓ make an attempt to explain why they react as they do?

Students are asked to read TallMountain's poem a second and a third time. When they've finished, they are to state their impressions of either the subject of the poem or the feelings it evokes in them.

READING AND WRITING EXTENSIONS

➤ Ask students to read, analyze, and then present a poem of their choice to the class. They should be prepared to lead a discussion about readers' first impressions of the poem.

➤ Ask students to write an opening paragraph that conveys a strong first impression of a character or a setting. Remind them to use figurative language and imagery in their writing.

Two Noticing Details

Critical Reading

FOCUS

Too often we read quickly and ignore the descriptive details an author has used to create an impression. It is important to focus on each description and visualize exactly what the author has described.

BACKGROUND

This lesson asks students to examine how the details an author includes in a piece of writing can help readers visualize the text. The excerpt from *Brave Men* is part of an article written in June 1944 by the American journalist Ernie Pyle, a noted war correspondent who became famous for his intimate accounts of soldiers at the front during World War II. In keeping with his usual style, Pyle focused his article on the human side of the conflict he had witnessed. In this article he offers a clear, highly detailed snapshot of a post-invasion Normandy beach.

➤ Notice Pyle's slow start in the article. He takes his time focusing his "lens"—he ponders the water's edge, he glances at the bodies floating in the surf, and then takes a moment to look at the "squishy little jellyfish" floating in the waves. Because he starts out so slowly, the reader is given a strong sense of his reluctance. We know that he's going to tell us about the carnage before him, but we also know that he doesn't want to, that he'd rather be almost anywhere than on this beach at this moment.

➤ As soon as Pyle focuses his lens, he begins to assault the reader with one painful image after another: " . . . there were abandoned rolls of barbed wire and smashed bulldozers and big stacks of thrown-away life belts . . . and empty life rafts and soldiers' packs and ration boxes, and mysterious oranges." Because Pyle never skimps on detail, we are given a remarkably clear view of the scene and are able to imagine the life-or-death struggle that took place there.

FOR DISCUSSION AND REFLECTION

Discuss with students how an author's use of details can set the scene, shape the tone, and contribute to the theme.

➤ Why is it important for a writer to use concrete rather than abstract details? (Concrete details place the reader firmly in the world of the story. Without them, an author will lose the reader.)

➤ What are some techniques a writer can use to organize details effectively? (Possible answers include arranging details as a description, making a comparison, describing cause and effect, giving evidence for a conclusion, classifying, putting in chronological order, or illustrating a point or idea.)

Writing

QUICK ASSESS

Do students' logs:

✓ reveal general and specific impressions of the text?

✓ demonstrate an understanding of how the details contribute to the piece?

Students are asked fill in a double-entry log designed to examine their impressions of Pyle's article. Before they begin, have students review the response notes they made in the margins of the text.

READING AND WRITING EXTENSIONS

➤ Have students write their own newspaper article in which they describe a scene or an event. Students may want to use Pyle's article as a model for their writing style.

➤ Ask students to write a paragraph that explains how Pyle's article is different from the articles published in today's newspapers.

Three Framing the Scene

Critical Reading

FOCUS

Pyle uses descriptions like the following to put his reader on the beachhead:

"The water was full of squishy little jellyfish about the size of a man's hand. Millions of them. In the center of each of them was a green design exactly like a four-leafed clover."

BACKGROUND

For "Framing the Scene," students are asked to read the Pyle excerpt again, this time watching for the ways Pyle seems to "zoom in" on certain aspects of the scene. Remind students that when Pyle wrote this article, there was no television. Newspaper readers on the home front relied on reporters like Pyle to tell them what they needed to know about the war, to make them a part of the action so that they could feel like they were fighting alongside their brothers, husbands, and sons.

➤ Notice how Pyle describes almost everything he sees. He doesn't take it for granted, for example, that his reader will know what jellyfish look like. He explains that they are squishy and little and each has a green design in the middle that is "exactly like a four-leafed clover." Although Pyle doesn't offer this much detail about everything he sees, he does give the reader enough detail to make it easy to form a mental picture of the scenery.

➤ Some aspects of the scene on the beach capture Pyle's interest more than others. He is the cameraman, so he gets to choose what we spend time looking at. For example, Pyle devotes a full three paragraphs to the soldiers' backpacks and the items that have fallen from them. In contrast, he never focuses on the dead soldiers themselves, though they are what Pyle's article is truly about.

FOR DISCUSSION AND REFLECTION

Discuss with students the value of forming lessons while we read.

➤ What techniques can writers use to help readers form these mental pictures? (Most mental images are formed by sensory details, which the author arranges in various ways.)

➤ How do our mental pictures affect our understanding of a piece of writing? (Answers will vary, but should focus on the necessity of visualizing what an author describes.)

Writing

QUICK ASSESS

Do students' pictures:

✓ focus on just one scene?

✓ depict the scene in some detail?

✓ reflect time, effort, and originality?

Students are asked to select one scene from Pyle's article and then draw what they "see." They might also write a sentence or two explaining how the scene makes them feel.

READING AND WRITING EXTENSIONS

➤ Have students check the library for newspaper articles about a more recent conflict. Ask them to choose an article they feel is well-written and then compare that article to Pyle's article on the Normandy invasion. Students' comparisons should focus on the differences in writing style, amount of detail, and kinds of detail offered.

➤ Ask students to turn Pyle's article into a short poem about the Normandy invasion. You might help them get started by brainstorming which details from the article might translate into strong poetic images.

Four Listening to the Text

Critical Reading

FOCUS

Good descriptions will appeal to all of our senses. Just as we listen when we watch a movie, we should also listen to the aural details of a text as we read.

BACKGROUND

An important part of visualizing a text is listening to how it "sounds." When we read, we often add sound effects to the descriptions. Some writers make it easy for a reader to add sound effects by using *onomatopoeia* in their writing. (Onomatopoeia is a word or words that imitate the sound of the thing spoken: *buzz, hum, cuckoo, splash.*) Other writers rely on vivid descriptions to help them conjure the *effect* of sound. In this excerpt from *Woodsong*, Gary Paulsen uses both techniques.

➤ Paulsen often uses onomatopoeia in order to add sound to his writing. At several points in his story, Paulsen pauses to describe what he hears: "I heard some whining and growling, then a scrabbling sound, and was amazed to see that he had taken the team back up the gully. . . ." Paulsen's pauses to interject sound are in no way a distraction from the smooth flow of the action. In fact, his use of onomatopoeia goes a long way toward holding the reader's interest while he explains what is happening.

➤ Another way Paulsen creates the effect of sound in his writing is by using vivid, highly detailed descriptions. Readers can't help but think about the sounds Paulsen heard (and made) as he fell down the gully, for example, or felt his knee pop out of place. At a couple of points he can't stop himself from grunting or moaning and he is quick to admit this to the reader.

FOR DISCUSSION AND REFLECTION

Discuss with students the reasons a reader might want to "hear" a story.

➤ How does the sound of a story contribute to its meaning? (Sound details give the impression of dimensionality to descriptions of setting.)

➤ What other kinds of writing do readers benefit from "hearing"? (Readers benefit from hearing any carefully written writing, particularly poetry.)

Writing

QUICK ASSESS

Can students:

✓ explain the sound effects and dialogue they've added to the Paulsen piece?

✓ evaluate whether their additions enhance or detract from the writing?

As a prewriting activity, students are asked to add dialogue and sound effects to the excerpt from *Woodsong*. Then students evaluate how the addition of sound effects changes their perspective on Paulsen's experience.

READING AND WRITING EXTENSIONS

➤ As an additional challenge, have students work together in small groups to add sound to the entire excerpt. When they've finished, they might present their work to the class in the form of a *Woodsong* radio broadcast.

➤ Invite students to read the rest of *Woodsong*—or another book by Gary Paulsen—and then report on it to the class. At least a part of students' reports should be devoted to analyzing Paulsen's style, language, and themes.

Five Making Mental Movies

Critical Reading

FOCUS

Sound needs to be studied very carefully when reading poetry. The rhythm and diction of a poem are essential elements in what the author is expressing.

BACKGROUND

After joining the Los Angeles Lakers in 1980, Magic Johnson spurred them on to the first of five NBA championships. During this period, the 6-ft. 9-in. Johnson won three Most Valuable Player awards. He had career averages of 19.7 points, 7.2 rebounds, and 11.4 assists per game.

➤ "Making Mental Movies" invites students to continue their exploration of the movies we create in our minds as we read. In this lesson, students are asked to think about the scenes they visualize and the audio they "hear" when they read poetry. Because its rhythm is so strong and its language is so vibrant, Quincy Troupe's "A Poem for 'Magic'" provides an excellent example of the kind of visualizing we are able to do when we read.

➤ Even though students may not know the poetic terms *rhythm* and *meter*, they certainly will be able to "hear" the beat of "A Poem for 'Magic.'" The rhythm of the poem, which mimics the rhythm of a bouncing basketball, creates a feeling of immediacy: we are there in the stands watching Magic's "magic."

➤ The language Troupe uses in his poem—his verb tenses, word choices, and imagery—also give readers the sense that they are a part of the action. Notice how Troupe writes in the present tense throughout the poem. His verbs make the poem read as a kind of rhythmic play-by-play that readers find interesting and engaging.

FOR DISCUSSION AND REFLECTION

Discuss with students the ways writers play with words and images to convey both audio and visual pictures.

➤ Is poetry an oral or a written art? (Opinions will vary, but students should discuss the oral origins of poetry and the fact that the basic elements of poetry—rhythm, rhyme, figures of speech—are oral techniques.)

➤ What are some techniques poets use to help readers make audio and visual pictures of their writing? (Possible answers include rhythm, word choice, syntax, and diction.)

Writing

QUICK ASSESS

Do students' poems:

✓ reflect an understanding of sound imagery and how it is used in poetry?

✓ reflect an understanding of visual imagery and how it is used in poetry?

Students are asked to write a poem that vividly describes a performer. As a prewriting activity, students create a word bank of sight and sound words.

READING AND WRITING EXTENSIONS

➤ Invite students to watch a tape of Magic Johnson (or another player) playing basketball. As they watch, students should jot down words that capture the action. Then have students write a paragraph comparing their own descriptive words to the words in Troupe's poem.

➤ Did other poets use the same kind of imagery Troupe uses in "A Poem for 'Magic'"? Did their poems invite readers to form mental movies? Ask students to choose a poet and research this question. Then report their findings to the class.

PERSPECTIVES ON A SUBJECT

Unit Overview

"Perspectives on a Subject: Baseball" explores a few of the many ways an author can approach a single topic. Students will examine point of view, perspective, and author's bias. In addition, they will consider how an author's perspective or bias can affect meaning. As a part of their examination of "shifting perspectives," students will consider the various perspectives a reader can bring to a piece of writing and how these perspectives can affect meaning.

LITERATURE FOCUS

Lesson	Literature
1. Finding a Topic	**Shirley Jackson**, from *Raising Demons* (Nonfiction)
2. Taking an Original Approach	**Annie Dillard**, from *An American Childhood* (Autobiography)
3. Developing a Topic Through a Portrait	**Sam Lacy**, "Hall of Famer Still on Cloud 9" (Nonfiction)
4. Developing a Topic Through Memories	**Ann Hood**, "Memoir" (Nonfiction)
5. Exploring the Significance of a Subject	**Roger Angell**, from "Celebration" (Nonfiction)

READING FOCUS

1. Understanding how writers focus on topics can help readers understand the structure and details of a story, poem, or essay.
2. Topics do not have to be original, but writers need to find a fresh approach or angle on the subject.
3. Reading about a person related to a subject provides a personal perspective on it and helps hold interest in your subject.
4. Some writers approach a subject through memories and personal feelings, using their experiences to reflect on an idea.
5. Searching for the significance of a subject can enlarge our understanding of it.

WRITING FOCUS

1. Write a summary of an author's perspective on a subject and examine the story's effect on your own perspective.
2. Explore concepts such as audience, main idea, purpose, and style from the perspective of the author.
3. Use a variety of characterization techniques to develop a character study of someone you know.
4. Write about the stories or connections that an author's memoir triggers for you.
5. Explore a baseball term by writing about the significance the term has outside the realm of baseball.

One Finding a Topic

Critical Reading

FOCUS

Shirley Jackson takes up the topic of baseball from how it affects the life of her family. It is a social rather than an atheletic perspective.

BACKGROUND

In "Finding a Topic," students will explore the variety of ways by which they can narrow a list of subjects down to just one topic. To help them see the difference between subjects and topics—and to help them see how very different individual perspectives on the same topic can be—they'll read an excerpt from Shirley Jackson's memoir, *Raising Demons*.

➤ You might begin by focusing students' attention on point of view. This is a first-person narrative told from the point of view of a mother who has become an active supporter of her town's Little League. As such, the reader is privy only to those aspects of baseball that this slightly harried mother sees. For example, instead of giving us a play-by-play description of a game, she tells us about the need to move the dinner hour so as not to interfere with practice.

➤ Students should also be aware of the close relationship between perspective and tone. Sometimes the tone of a piece is so significant that it alone can bring freshness to a topic. In the case of this excerpt, the tone helps give the subject of baseball a fresh or different look. Notice how the mother rushes here and there, cooking, fundraising, gossiping, and so on. Because the mother is a bit harried, the narrative has a rushed, tell-the-story-quickly feel to it.

FOR DISCUSSION AND REFLECTION

Discuss with students how the Jackson piece would be different if the perspective were changed.

➤ How does the mother's perspective affect the tone of the story? (Students might describe the tone as humorous, amused, harried, or surprised.)

➤ How might the story change if it were told by Laurie's father? (Answers will vary based on students' experiences and images of fathers.)

Writing

QUICK ASSESS

Do students' summaries:

✔ identify characteristics of Jackson's perspective?

✔ explain how Jackson's perspective affected their attitudes toward baseball?

Students are asked to write a two- or three-sentence summary of Jackson's perspective on baseball. As a prewriting activity, they'll be asked to make a cluster that explores Jackson's subjects and details.

READING AND WRITING EXTENSIONS

➤ Ask students to retell this story from the perspective of Laurie, the little boy who will play for the Little League Braves. Their retelling of the story should be at least one page in length.

➤ Have students write a one-paragraph character sketch of this Little League mother. Encourage them to describe what they think she looks like, talks like, and thinks about.

Two Taking an Original Approach

Critical Reading

FOCUS

Annie Dillard on writing: "When you write, you lay out a line of words. The line of words is a miner's pick, a woodcarver's gouge, a surgeon's probe. Soon you find yourself deep in a new territory...."

BACKGROUND

In this lesson students will be asked to consider the many different ways a writer can approach a single subject. Although writers are not necessarily obligated to find original subjects to write about, they *are* obligated to offer readers a fresh perspective on a given subject. In this excerpt from her autobiography, *An American Childhood,* award-winning author Annie Dillard takes a fresh approach to the subject of baseball.

➤ Dillard's angle on the subject of baseball involves describing the sport from the perspective of one who loves the game but is deliberately excluded from playing. Dillard's perspective is unique because it's not often that we stop to consider how it feels to be on the sidelines, rather than in the center of the action.

➤ We can tell from her writing that Dillard is interested in conveying the envy and frustration she felt when she watched the players play. Throughout her essay she uses sensory language to help us experience her anguish. We sympathize when her heart cracks along with the crack of the bat, just as we can feel her longing to catch a baseball in her mitt where it would stay ". . . snap, like a mouse locked in its trap, not like some pumpkin of a softball you merely halted, with a terrible sound like a splat."

FOR DISCUSSION AND REFLECTION

Discuss with students the author's point of view in this story.

➤ What is the tone of the writing? (Students might describe the tone or mood as envious, frustrated, yearning, serious, or respectful.)

➤ What techniques does Dillard use to get the audience to see her point of view? (Possible answers include sensory language, vivid details, strong comparisons, and a serious tone.)

Writing

QUICK ASSESS

Do students' answers:

✓ consistently maintain Dillard's point of view?

✓ discuss Dillard's main idea?

✓ demonstrate understanding of the author's purpose?

Students are asked to answer a series of questions from Annie Dillard's perspective. The questions concern the ways in which Dillard accommodated her audience as she wrote the piece.

READING AND WRITING EXTENSIONS

➤ Ask students to write a personal narrative about a time they felt left out. How do their feelings about the event differ from Dillard's feelings?

➤ Have students compare and contrast Dillard's perspective on baseball to Jackson's perspective on baseball. What are some similarities and differences?

Three Developing a Topic Through a Portrait

Critical Reading

FOCUS

A writer can take a fresh approach to a topic such as baseball by writing about a person—a coach, player, or owner, for example—associated with the game.

BACKGROUND

Yet another way of offering readers a fresh angle on a topic is to approach the topic from the perspective of its personalities. To help them explore the ways a writer can develop a character study related to a subject, students will read a newspaper article written by Sam Lacy of the *Baltimore Afro-American*.

➤ Notice that although this is a news article about Jackie Robinson's induction into baseball's Hall of Fame, Lacy maintains a focus on character, rather than on the highlights of Robinson's career. For example, Lacy tells the reader that Robinson spoke "in a voice that betrayed an inward battle to hold back the tears." He doesn't mention, however, that Robinson helped lead the Dodgers to six pennants.

➤ Lacy paints a flesh-and-blood portrait of Robinson in other ways as well. He makes a point of quoting Robinson's fans as often as he quotes baseball professionals such as Branch Rickey. And he shows us that Robinson is a family man who wants his three children with him when he accepts his award.

FOR DISCUSSION AND REFLECTION

Discuss with students the characteristics of a portrait or character study.

➤ Why do you think Lacy chose to write a character study of Robinson rather than a standard news story about the ceremony? (A character study is more personal, emotional, and interesting.)

➤ What are some techniques an author uses in a character study? (Possible answers include description, anecdotes, and quotations.)

Writing

QUICK ASSESS

Do the character sketches:

✔ reveal character through direct description?

✔ include information about the character's words and/or actions?

✔ reveal character through the words/actions of others?

Students are asked to describe a person they know. As a prewriting activity, they'll examine the Lacy article for his techniques of characterization.

READING AND WRITING EXTENSIONS

➤ Ask students to research and then write about a sports star they admire. Before they begin, they might want to review the different techniques for developing character (page 72).

➤ Have students return to the descriptions they wrote about a person they know. Ask them to delete all physical description from their paragraphs and rely instead on dialogue and action as a means of revealing character.

➤ Invite students to thumb through their literature anthologies to find examples of the various ways authors reveal characters. Have them summarize their findings in a paragraph.

Four **Developing a Topic Through Memories**

C r i t i c a l   R e a d i n g

FOCUS

Ann Hood on baseball:

"Baseball is in my blood. Like the light hair and eyes I inherited from my father, and the hot Italian temper I got from my mother, a love of baseball runs through my veins."

Sometimes authors will explore a topic through memories and personal feelings.

BACKGROUND

Another way that writers can provide a new perspective on a topic is to explore the topic through the lens of their own memories, thoughts, and personal feelings. As an example of the ways in which an author's autobiographical perspective can bring a fresh viewpoint to a familiar subject, students will read from Ann Hood's memoir of her life as a baseball-lover.

➤ As Hood explores her experiences and memories of baseball, her perspective is hers and hers alone. She cannot, for example, explain how Butch Hobson felt as the fans lined up to see him at the mall, just as she cannot explain what her father was thinking as he watched the game with his daughter at his side.

➤ Notice how thorough Hood is in describing the ways in which the game of baseball has affected her. She begins her memoir by telling us that she adores the sport, though she's not quite sure why. She goes on to explain the effect baseball has had on her feelings about herself, her feelings about her father, her relationships with men, even her conversations with strangers at a wedding.

FOR DISCUSSION AND REFLECTION

Discuss with students how their own memories, thoughts, and feelings about baseball affect their reading of Hood's memoir.

➤ Which of Hood's experiences seem familiar to students? (Responses will vary.)

➤ How does a reader's familiarity with a topic affect the reading experience? (Familiarity with a topic makes it more accessible, can trigger personal memories, and helps readers connect the topic with their own experiences.)

W r i t i n g

QUICK ASSESS

Does students' writing:

✓ explore the ways in which they connect to Hood's memoir?

✓ describe stories or memories of their own that link to Hood's memoir?

Students are asked to write about the stories or connections Hood's memoir triggers for them.

READING AND WRITING EXTENSIONS

➤ Invite students to write a letter from Ann Hood to Shirley Jackson, Annie Dillard, or Sam Lacy. What would Hood like to say to these other baseball fans?

➤ Have students write an essay about baseball. Remind them that they'll need to offer a fresh perspective on the sport. If they need to, students can do an online or a periodical search for baseball topics of interest.

Five Exploring the Significance of a Subject

Critical Reading

FOCUS

Roger Angell on baseball:

"Sometimes I think baseball was invented just to remind us of things. It's a living memory, and it has an epic quality—you can't get away from it."

Reflecting on a subject and its significance can sometimes lead us to a new understanding of it.

BACKGROUND

Sometimes talking about a subject or spending time researching a subject can help an author discover a new angle or a new perspective. Many writers spend time brainstorming ideas with others to help sharpen their focus on a topic. Other writers spend time researching or reflecting in the hopes that a new perspective will present itself.

➤ In his essay "Celebration," Roger Angell and a group of friends sift through what they know about baseball and eventually arrive at a new understanding of what the sport means to them. During their conversation, they analyze baseball's specialized language ("bullpen," "home plate"), its rituals of behavior, and the traditions associated with the game. As they work through the topic, they suggest several ideas about baseball that hadn't occurred to them before.

➤ Notice how, as the men in the car talk, they widen the focus of the conversation from the narrow topic of baseball vocabulary to the wider topic of baseball as a metaphor for the struggle of human existence. For example, they compare a "run" to humankind's tendency to keep trying, even in the face of serious obstacles.

FOR DISCUSSION AND REFLECTION

Discuss with students the different kinds of specialized language we use in English.

➤ How does specialized language differ from standard English? (Specialized terms are used and understood within a special context and by a specific group of people.)

➤ Why do you think baseball terminology has become part of our everyday speech? (Possible answer: Baseball is so much a part of American culture that its terminology has become familiar, popular, and widely used.)

Writing

QUICK ASSESS

Do students' paragraphs:

✓ offer a definition of the term?

✓ suggest possible origins for the term?

✓ discuss the significance of the term in a larger context?

Students are asked to write a paragraph in which they explain the significance of a baseball term such as "home plate." In their paragraphs they'll explain the significance the term has beyond the world of baseball.

READING AND WRITING EXTENSIONS

➤ Invite students to search for another example of baseball writing. Have them present what they find to the class and explain the ways in which the author offers a fresh perspective.

➤ Ask students to think about another subject area that has its own unique vocabulary. (Consider, for example, the extensive vocabulary associated with computer use: "online," "byte," "Net," and so on.) Have students write an essay on the subject and the significance of its vocabulary.

THE UNIVERSE OF LANGUAGE

Unit Overview

In "The Universe of Language," students explore the idea that we define our world with words. What we say (and how we say it) can reveal to others our perceptions of ourselves and our perceptions of the world around us. Students will examine the "wordmaps" of three different authors: Eve Merriam, Alice Walker, and May Swenson. Students will be invited to make wordmaps of their own and then think about the ways their vocabulary and language reveal their views of the world.

LITERATURE FOCUS

Lesson	Literature
1. Discovering a Universe of Language	**Eve Merriam**, "Thumbprint" (Poetry)
2. Mapping Your Universe	
3. Working with Words	
4. A Universe in a Story	**Alice Walker**, "The Flowers" (Short Story)
5. The Heart of the Matter	**May Swenson**, "The Universe" (Poetry)

READING FOCUS

1. Words are sensory and authors choose them carefully to reflect the way we perceive the world with our five senses.
2. Thinking visually with words can help us understand how we perceive the world and what words mean to us.
3. Working with words helps you understand how they can be used to express your thoughts, feelings, and sensations.
4. By looking closely at a writer's universe of words, we can better understand what the writer values and how he or she sees the world.
5. Words express our personalities and values. Understanding words and their nuances can help us understand what writers are trying to say.

WRITING FOCUS

1. Explore the idea of a personal "universe of language" by listing and classifying words.
2. Make a map or drawing that reflects your universe of language.
3. Write a poem that uses words from your universe of language and shows how the words are related.
4. Analyze how an author's use of sensory language and action words affect the meaning of a story.
5. Review, modify, and reflect on your personal universe of language.

One Discovering a Universe of Language

Critical Reading

FOCUS

Eve Merriam on poetry:

"I think one is chosen to be a poet. You write poems because you must write them; because you can't live your life without writing them."

BACKGROUND

In "Discovering a Universe of Language," students will explore how the words we use help define what we think and feel, and how we see the world. In her poem "Thumbprint," Eve Merriam has an interesting way of exploring the idea that every person is completely unique: she focuses on our thumbprints and celebrates the well-known fact that no two fingerprints are the same.

➤ Notice how Merriam uses her thumbprint as a metaphor for everything that makes her unique. The whorls on her thumb are hers alone, just as her identity, her feelings, her thoughts and dreams are hers and hers alone: "I am myself, /of all my atom parts I am the sum."

➤ In the second part Merriam extends the metaphor by telling us that she turns the pages of the universe with her thumb, that she can "Imprint [her] mark upon the world. . . ." In other words, just as her thumbprint is completely unique, so are her hopes, thoughts, and dreams. She is prepared to show the world who she is, and will welcome the individuality of others.

FOR DISCUSSION AND REFLECTION

Discuss with students how Merriam's word choices affect the tone and meaning of her poem.

➤ What is the predominant mood of the poem? What is the tone? (Both the mood and tone are celebratory.)

➤ Which of the senses do the images in the poem primarily appeal to? (The images appeal to the sense of touch.)

➤ Judging from this poem, what does Eve Merriam value? How do you know? (She values the individual. She expresses this value both literally and figuratively.)

Writing

QUICK ASSESS

Are students' wordmaps:

✓ complete?

✓ detailed?

✓ thoughtfully done?

Students are asked to begin the process of classifying and describing their vocabularies. Working individually, they will create their own wordmaps.

READING AND WRITING EXTENSIONS

➤ Have students exchange wordmaps with a partner. After they've read their partner's wordmap, they should write a paragraph in which they summarize their partner's vocabulary thumbprint.

➤ As a class, brainstorm a list of well-known people (entertainers, politicians, sports figures, and so on) who have highly distinctive wordmaps. Ask students to choose one person on the list to research and then write about in a journal entry.

Two Mapping Your Universe

Critical Reading

BACKGROUND

Discuss with students the ways in which their wordmaps are unique. Ask for volunteers to photocopy their maps and then distribute them to the class. Are there any words common to many students' maps? If so, discuss why. When you have finished analyzing students' wordmaps, invite the class to begin work on "Mapping Your Universe." This lesson asks students to continue their exploration of vocabulary thumbprints by making a visual representation of their wordmaps. Students will use their words to create a design that reflects the ways they perceive the world.

FOR DISCUSSION AND REFLECTION

Discuss with students the ways in which our vocabularies can reveal information about our perceptions of the world.

➤ What are some aspects of spoken language that give listeners clues about who we are? (Possible answers include vocabulary, accent and other regional differences, volume, and tempo.)

➤ What can our vocabulary thumbprints reveal about us? (Our language can give listeners clues about where we're from, our culture, education, perceptions, and attitudes.)

Writing

QUICK ASSESS
Do students' drawings:

✓ clearly represent their perceptions of the world?

✓ incorporate the wordmaps they created for Lesson One?

✓ show effort, creativity, and careful planning?

For this activity students will turn their wordmaps into images. You might spend a few minutes discussing with students some of the suggestions listed on page 83 of their books.

READING AND WRITING EXTENSIONS

➤ For an interesting activity, gather all the students' designs into a pile and shuffle them. Show each design to the class without revealing the artist's name. Ask students to guess who created the picture. How well do they know the language thumbprints of their classmates?

➤ Invite students to make a wordmap or drawing of Eve Merriam's universe of language. Have them begin by studying her vocabulary in "Thumbprint." Later they can check the library for other examples of Merriam's writing and use those examples to supplement what they know about Merriam's use of language.

Three Working with Words

Critical Reading

FOCUS
Oscar Wilde on crafting poetry: "A poet can survive anything but a misprint."

BACKGROUND

Now that students have spent some time thinking about how their vocabularies reflect their perceptions of the world, it's time for them to begin thinking about the ways we *communicate* those perceptions to others. In "Working with Words," students are asked to write a poem that reveals their thoughts and feelings about the world around them.

➤ Discuss with students how the language they use in their poems—the word choices they make, the images they evoke—can effectively convey their messages. For example, Eve Merriam doesn't need to say in her poem "Every person is unique." Her thumbprint metaphor conveys this message in a much more poetic and meaningful way.

➤ You may also want to review with students what they know about poetic structure. Remind them that although not all poetry rhymes, every poem needs some kind of rhythm, be it regular or irregular. The rhythm of the poem is its beat. Only free verse (poetry written with rhythm and other poetic devices but no fixed pattern of meter and rhyme) has an irregular rhythm.

FOR DISCUSSION AND REFLECTION

Discuss with students what our language can reveal about our thoughts, our feelings, and our views of the world.

➤ What are some of the environmental factors that can affect a person's universe of language? (Our universe of language is affected by cultural and regional differences, and differences in education, age, and economics.)

➤ What aspects of poetry are most important in helping to convey the poet's meaning? (Possible answers include word choice, tone, rhythm, and structure.)

Writing

QUICK ASSESS

Do students' poems:

✔ use words from their wordmaps?

✔ reflect an understanding of poetic form?

✔ reflect a creative use of language?

Students are asked to write a poem using the words from their wordmaps. As a prewriting activity, students will sort and group words in a chart.

READING AND WRITING EXTENSIONS

➤ Have each student look at his or her poem. What do they like best about the poem? What do they like least? What would they do differently the next time?

➤ Have the class write a round-robin poem about language. Ask a volunteer to supply the first line and then move around the room collecting one line from each student. Have someone record the lines as you go.

Four A Universe in a Story

Critical Reading

FOCUS

Alice Walker on why she writes:

"I'm really paying homage to the people I love, the people who are thought to be dumb and backward but who were the ones who first taught me to see beauty."

BACKGROUND

In "A Universe in a Story," students are invited to read and respond to Alice Walker's powerful short story "Flowers." As they read, students should watch for the ways Walker uses language—her personal wordmap—to direct the reader's responses to the scenes.

➤ One of the ways Walker directs the reader's response to her story is by using sensory language. Because she takes the time to describe what Myop sees, feels, hears, and smells on her journey, Walker is able to cajole the reader into sharing Myop's pleasure in the day.

➤ Another way Walker directs the reader's response is by placing a heavy emphasis on mood. Notice the mood of the first four paragraphs of the story. The language Walker uses is light and carefree—as light and carefree, in fact, as a girl for whom nothing exists "but her song, the stick clutched in her dark brown hand, and the tat-de-ta-ta of accompaniment." The sudden change of mood in paragraph five foreshadows Myop's discovery of the dead man's body. Once she has established the change in mood, Walker can devote the rest of her story to revealing the message she has for her readers.

FOR DISCUSSION AND REFLECTION

Discuss with students how writers' wordmaps relate to the mood and meaning of their stories.

➤ What words and phrases in the beginning of "The Flowers" convey a mood that is light and carefree? (Possible answers include: "skipped lightly," "the days had never been as beautiful as these," "a golden surprise," "light and good.")

➤ What words and phrases signify a change to a darker, more sinister mood? (Possible answers include: "strangeness of the land," "not as pleasant as her usual haunts," "gloomy," "silence close and deep.")

Writing

QUICK ASSESS

Do students' explanations:

✔ reflect an understanding of the underlying message of Walker's story?

✔ reflect an understanding of the characteristics of sensory language?

Students are asked to analyze and explain how Walker's sensory language and action words affect the meaning of the story. As a prewriting activity, students will complete a word chart.

READING AND WRITING EXTENSIONS

➤ Ask students to complete a sensory and action word chart for a poem of their choice. Have them do the same for a newspaper article. Then have them compare these two charts with the chart for Walker's short story. What generalizations can they make about sensory language?

➤ Invite students to perform a dramatic reading of "Flowers." How does an oral reading of the story affect students' opinion about Walker's use of language?

Five The Heart of the Matter

Critical Reading

FOCUS

May Swenson on poetry:

[Poetry is] "based on a craving to get through the curtains of things as they *appear*, to things as they *are*, and then into the larger, wilder space of things as they are *becoming*."

A frequently anthologized American poet, May Swenson (1919–1989) spent hours listening to the "sound" of her language.

BACKGROUND

In "The Heart of the Matter" students are reminded that when it comes to language, individual words are not nearly so important as how a person puts those words together. Writers choose words that will help them achieve the effect they're looking for and reveal the meaning they're trying to get across. May Swenson, a poet with a reputation for highly evocative glimpses of nature and everyday life, almost always used the bare minimum of words in her poetry. Because her style was spare, Swenson was extremely careful to choose exactly the right word or phrase.

➤ Notice how Swenson uses many of the same words over and over again in her poem. Notice also the *kinds* of words Swenson tends to repeat. Although many poets use repetition, most poets wouldn't choose weak words such as "what," "about," and "because" to repeat. Swenson does repeat these kinds of words, to great effect.

➤ In a roundabout way, Swenson's word choices contribute to her underlying meaning in the poem. This poem explores the complex theme of our role in the infinite universe in a refreshingly simple, almost childlike way. By using simple language, Swenson is able to make a complex, intimidating theme more accessible to her readers.

FOR DISCUSSION AND REFLECTION

Ask students why it is important to try to understand the nuances of the words a writer uses.

➤ How does a word's connotation differ from its meaning? (A word's connotation includes an emotional component—associations, memories, etc.)

➤ Why do writers choose words that have connotations? (Words that make an emotional connection affect readers more strongly and create a more memorable impression.)

Writing

QUICK ASSESS

Do students' responses:

✓ identify the words to be added to or deleted from their lists?

✓ discuss how these words reflect their views of the world?

Students are asked to review and modify the universe of language lists they made for this unit. Then, they will explain how the words on their lists reflect their worlds.

READING AND WRITING EXTENSIONS

➤ Invite students to compare and contrast Eve Merriam's "Thumbprint" to May Swenson's "The Universe." Students' comparisons should focus on these authors' use of language.

➤ Work with students to create a wordmap that reflects your school's universe of language. What words and phrases are popular with students? Which words do students think will be "crossed off" the school wordmap soon because they are going out of style?

THE POWER OF LANGUAGE

Unit Overview

In "The Power of Language" students will further their exploration of language by considering what our vocabularies reveal about us and the reasons why we might want to increase our language power. They will learn how to use details and concrete language in their writing. They will also learn about the power of figurative language and how it can help others visualize our ideas.

LITERATURE FOCUS

Lesson	Literature
1. Making an Abstraction Concrete	
2. Reading and Making Metaphors	**Sylvia Plath**, "Metaphors" (Poetry)
	Linda Pastan, "Camouflage" (Poetry)
3. Five-Finger Exercises	
4. The Power of the Word	**Wilfred Funk and Norman Lewis** from *Thirty Days to a More Powerful Vocabulary* (Nonfiction)
	Nalungiaq, "Magic Words" (Poetry)
5. To Make Life a Marvel	**Octavio Paz**, "Between What I See and What I Say..." (Poetry)

READING FOCUS

1. Good writers turn abstract ideas into powerful images by using concrete details to describe them.

2. A metaphor is a thoughtful comparison between two things. Writers use them to make us look at something in a new way.

3. Writers sometimes use writing exercises to unlock their creativity by forcing themselves to use a particular form or structure.

4. The power of language goes beyond time and culture; our words convey our personal universes.

5. The reader of poetry must stay with an image or an idea and read between the lines to fully understand a poet's power of language.

WRITING FOCUS

1. Describe an abstract image concretely, without using the word itself.

2. Write a riddle poem modeled after Sylvia Plath and interpret the use of similes and metaphors.

3. Practice poetic techniques by writing exercise poems.

4. Compare and contrast two pieces of writing and the authors' viewpoints on language.

5. Describe how you view poetry, responding to Octavio Paz's ideas.

One Making an Abstraction Concrete

Critical Reading

FOCUS

The poet May Swenson on sensory language:

"By bringing into play the sensual apparatus of the reader, the poem causes him to realize the content eye-wise, ear-wise, taste, touch, and muscle-wise before beginning to cerebralize."

BACKGROUND

Reading is a waste of time if we can't understand what the writer is saying. If the writer's vocabulary is too remote, or the sentences too complex, or the images too abstract, no reader will be able to understand what the writer is trying to say. In "Making an Abstraction Concrete," students will explore ways to make an abstraction concrete enough for readers to get hold of it.

➤ The easiest way to make an abstraction concrete is through the use of sensory language. If we are given something we can touch, hear, taste, see, or even smell, it is easier for us to understand the underlying abstraction.

➤ Usually an abstraction can be represented by any number of concrete images. The abstraction *freedom*, for example, can be made concrete by describing a set of broken manacles (touch), a copy of the Declaration of Independence (sight), *The Battle Hymn of the Republic* (hearing), or the college dining hall on your first day away from home (smell).

FOR DISCUSSION AND REFLECTION

Discuss with students why concrete images make our writing more powerful.

➤ Why is it that readers find sensory language easy to understand? (Sensory language appeals immediately to our sense of taste, sound, sight, smell, and touch.)

➤ What types of writing rely the most on sensory details? (Poetry is the literary form that relies the most on sensory details. Nonfiction pieces rely on sensory details as well to help you visualize people or places.)

Writing

QUICK ASSESS

Do students:

✓ use sensory language to describe their abstractions?

✓ succeed in making their abstractions concrete?

Students are asked to write a description of an abstraction without using the abstraction itself. As a prewriting activity, they draw a picture of the abstraction.

READING AND WRITING EXTENSIONS

➤ As an additional challenge, invite students to write a poem about an abstraction that interests them. Remind them to use sensory language to make the abstraction concrete.

➤ Ask students to gather several examples of different kinds of writing (news articles, poems, short stories, and so on) and then examine the amount and the kind of symbolism used in each type of writing. They can take notes on what they find. Is there a kind of writing that never (or rarely) uses symbolism? Is there a type of writing that uses quite a lot of it?

Two Reading and Making Metaphors

Critical Reading

FOCUS

Although we use metaphors in conversation without thinking about them (for example, "time flies"), many writers still find it difficult to use metaphors in their writing. A metaphor is a comparison between two basically unlike things and can also be tricky to identify.

BACKGROUND

Lesson Two, "Reading and Making Metaphors," helps students understand how to identify a metaphor in a piece of writing and how to add metaphors to their own writing. Sylvia Plath's "Metaphors" and Linda Pastan's "Camouflage" both include metaphors that are easy to find and some that require a little extra thought.

➤ In "Metaphors," Plath presents her readers with a riddle. Each line of her poem is a clue (in nine syllables, as promised). After a few readings it should be obvious that she is describing pregnancy in a unique way. Actually, a metaphor is often just that: a unique way of thinking about something that is complex or abstract. Think again about "time flies." The concept of time, which is highly abstract, becomes accessible when we compare it to a bird.

➤ Linda Pastan's poem "Camouflage" is also a kind of study of metaphors, but a more subtle one. In addition to providing students with an explanation of the differences between similes and metaphors, Pastan offers another example of how metaphors can bring freshness and vividness to writing. How many of us have ever thought to describe a facial expression as "smiles chainlinked across bone"?

FOR DISCUSSION AND REFLECTION

Discuss with students the effect a metaphor can have on our writing.

➤ Why does a writer use metaphors? (Writers generally use metaphors to describe something complex in more simple terms or as a way to surprise readers with a fresh description of a common object.)

➤ What are some of the problems associated with using metaphors? (Sometimes the implied comparison in a metaphor is difficult for the reader to follow. We all understand how "time flies," but "My love is like a red, red rose" is confusing without the explanation of the rest of the poem.)

Writing

QUICK ASSESS

Do students:

✓ understand the characteristics of a metaphor?

✓ understand the difference between similes and metaphors?

Students are asked to complete two activities in this lesson. First they will write a riddle poem using Plath's poem as a model. Next they will analyze the first four lines of Pastan's poem in terms of what she reveals about similes and metaphors.

READING AND WRITING EXTENSIONS

➤ Ask students to work as a class to make a list of old, tired metaphors that should be avoided.

➤ Ask students to write a paragraph in which they use at least two different metaphors to describe a favorite person, place, or thing.

Three Five-Finger Exercises

Critical Reading

FOCUS

Practice is essential to developing a strong writing style. Playing with forms will help you develop the skills to write interestingly and clearly.

BACKGROUND

A writer needs constant practice in the same way a gymnast or a singer does. "Five-Finger Exercises" shows students one way of practicing writing. In this lesson students will focus on writing different kinds of practice poems. Instead of allowing their creativity to run wild, however, they'll be asked to follow somewhat rigid poetic forms.

➤ In the first exercise, students are asked to describe an abstraction in five lines. As they write, they must pay attention to the restrictions on word count.

➤ In the second exercise, students are asked to write a five-line description of an object. Each line must contain a metaphor.

➤ In the third exercise, students are asked to create a three-line fulcrum poem—the poetic equivalent of a see-saw. Two lines of three words are balanced and connected by one central word.

➤ In the fourth exercise, students are asked to write an alliteration poem using one line with five words. Remind students that alliteration is the repetition of consonant sounds at the beginnings of words or accented syllables: "A sinewy snake slithered slowly through the stable."

➤ In the fifth exercise, students are invited to take a word for a "walk." They will use the same word once in every line of a six-line poem. The trick for students will be to use the word in the location specified in their *Daybooks*.

FOR DISCUSSION AND REFLECTION

Discuss with students what they found most difficult about the five-finger poetic exercises.

➤ Which poetic form was most challenging? Why? (Responses will vary.)

➤ How do exercises like the ones students just completed help writers unlock their creativity? (These sorts of exercises help a writer to develop a strong style and technique, which allows them to focus on what they want to say and how they are expressing it.)

Writing

QUICK ASSESS

Do students' poems:

✔ correctly follow the forms given?

✔ show an understanding of how to use metaphors?

✔ reflect careful thought and creativity?

Students are asked to write five poems using different poetic forms.

READING AND WRITING EXTENSIONS

➤ As an additional challenge, invite students to come up with a set of "five-finger" exercises another kind of writer might use—a playwright, for example, or a newspaper reporter. Have them write a set of directions explaining the exercise. When they are finished, students might present their exercises to the class.

➤ Have students evaluate what they have learned thus far about writing metaphors. In a paragraph, students should explain whether or not they now find it easier to write a metaphor. Do they feel any more confident about being able to spot a metaphor in a piece of writing? Why or why not?

Four The Power of the Word

Critical Reading

FOCUS

Our world is defined and shaped by words. "Without words you could make no decisions and form no judgments whatsoever."

BACKGROUND

In Lesson Four, "The Power of the Word," students are asked to consider the effect our vocabularies have on others. To help them do so, they read two markedly different pieces of writing: an excerpt from *Thirty Days to a More Powerful Vocabulary* and a poem by Nalungiaq. As they read, students should watch for the differences in what the two authors have to say about the power of language.

➤ Consider Funk's and Lewis's tone in the excerpt. They are serious, strident, and determined. Words are tools, and Funk and Lewis plan to use them skillfully. It's difficult to argue with the individual points, though readers may have a harder time agreeing that they "have *no other* medium for telling us [their] thoughts—for convincing us, persuading us, giving us orders."

➤ Nalungiaq would certainly agree that words are power, but he is convinced that we have other tools at our disposal to aid in communication. Nalungiaq is equally certain that the words we do use can do more than merely communicate our thoughts: "A word spoken by chance / might have strange consequences." How is what he says in his poem different from what Funk and Lewis say?

FOR DISCUSSION AND REFLECTION

Discuss with students the various ways we can improve our language skills.

➤ Why would we want to improve the way we talk? (Some responses: to increase comprehensibility, add style and polish to speaking ability, or allow us a wider range of expression.)

➤ What does our vocabulary reveal about us? (It can reveal many things, including geographic origin, level of education, profession or interests, social milieu, attitudes, etc.)

Writing

QUICK ASSESS
Are students' comparisons:

✔ clearly written?

✔ easy to follow?

✔ enjoyable to read?

Students are asked to compare and contrast the writings by Funk and Lewis and Nalungiaq. Students should comment on the effectiveness of the two pieces and whether or not they agree with both.

READING AND WRITING EXTENSIONS

➤ As an additional challenge, have students compare the Nalungiaq poem to the Pastan poem of Lesson Two. Students' comparisons should explore differences and similarities in language usage.

➤ Ask for a volunteer to perform a dramatic reading of Nalungiaq's poem. After the reading, have students write down three words that they think capture the essence of Nalungiaq's poem. When they've finished, invite students to explain their choices.

Five To Make Life a Marvel

Critical Reading

FOCUS

Octavio Paz wrote that "the mission of poetry is to create among people the possibility of wonder...."

BACKGROUND

In Lesson Five, students are asked to contemplate the role of poetry in the world. Octavio Paz's poem, "Between What I See and What I Say..." is a playful attempt to define poetry. The poem also demonstrates Paz's premise that the role of poetry is to make life a marvel. And if poetry is to make life a marvel, it must itself be something marvelous.

➤ Notice how in his tentative definitions of poetry Paz repeatedly makes use of paradox: "says / what I keep silent, / keeps silent / what I say," The Oxford English Dictionary defines paradox as "a statement contrary to received belief, often with the implication that it is marvelous." Paz's poem is a series of seeming contradictions which—upon reflection—make perfect sense: "Eyes speak, / words look / looks think. / To hear / thoughts, / see / what we say." Only an accomplished writer can carry off such word play.

➤ In the passage where Paz expresses his opinion of poetry and poets, he debunks the idea that poets are angels who walk the earth. Instead he describes them as transmitters, conduits for a kind of spiritual light that humans need to thrive.

FOR DISCUSSION AND REFLECTION

Ask students to list the many seeming contradictions (paradoxes) in "Between What I See and What I Say..."

➤ Discuss the effect Paz's placement of words on the page has on their reading. Speculate upon why the poet may have chosen to line out the poem in this manner. (It creates movement on the page, the line becomes a kind of balance beam, and it invites the reader to weigh two ideas at once.)

Writing

QUICK ASSESS

Have students:

✓ understood Paz's critique of a society that exiles poets?

✓ seen how poetry can be a kind of "light" in the world?

Students are asked to respond to Paz's observation that poets in the United States are not at the center of American society but in exile. To help them get started, ask students to think of times and places where poets and poetry have intersected with their lives. Have these occasions seemed central or peripheral?

READING AND WRITING EXTENSIONS

➤ Ask students to imagine a society where the president was a poet. Describe how this might affect that society's economy, politics, entertainment industry, or sports world. Turn this description into a poem.

➤ Invite students to write a poem of their own in which they make generous use of paradox to define an abstract concept: love, terror, speed, home. They might enjoy working with partners for these poems.

Unit Overview

In this cluster, students will explore the world of science fiction and fantasy through the writing of Ursula K. Le Guin. As they immerse themselves in her work, students will look at the characteristics of Le Guin's imaginary worlds, discuss elements of realism in her stories, and test their skills at writing their own science fiction.

LITERATURE FOCUS

Lesson	Literature
1. The Believing Game	from *The Eye of the Heron* (Novel)
2. A Story in Ten Words	from "The Kerastion" (Short Story)
3. Truth in Fantasy	from "Darkness Box" (Short Story)
4. A Tissue of Lies	
5. Dancing at the Edge of the World	from "World-Making" (Nonfiction)

READING FOCUS

1. In fantasy or thought experiment stories, the writer convinces the reader to believe that the fantasy elements of the story are somehow right and reasonable.

2. Writers of fantasy create imaginary objects that add layers of imagining to their work.

3. Authors often use realistic elements to make their imaginary worlds more believable.

4. Writers use familiar concepts and details as a way of grounding readers in reality. That way, the fictional world connects to the world with which readers are familiar.

5. Knowing about an author's interests and reasons for writing can help the reader understand the larger meaning behind the stories.

WRITING FOCUS

1. Design a book cover that captures the imaginary world of Le Guin's novel.

2. Describe a fantastical object in ten words, then incorporate the object into the beginning of a story.

3. Complete a series of sentences that examine fantasy, reality, and meaning in Le Guin's work.

4. Write a paragraph that describes and analyzes how realistic elements are extrapolated in Le Guin's writing.

5. Write a letter that offers advice about how to approach the reading of science fiction and fantasy.

One The Believing Game

Critical Reading

FOCUS

In *The Eye of the Heron,* Ursula K. Le Guin includes both familiar and fantastic elements in her description of a landscape:

"Across the river the forest rolled on southward in endless interlocking ring patterns under hanging clouds. Eastward, upriver, the land rose steeply; to the west the river wound in gray levels between lower hills."

BACKGROUND

A writer of fantasy creates another world for readers, one that exists only within the confines of a book or a set of books. An important part of a fantasy writer's job is to make that fantasy world credible. There need to be elements of realism in a fantasy; otherwise, readers will find it impossible to "suspend disbelief" and ignore the rules of the known world. One of the reasons Ursula K. Le Guin is so popular with adults and young adults alike is because she understands this balance between fantasy and reality. The worlds she creates in her books are brilliant blends of the fantastic and the believable, the imaginative and the everyday.

➤ Consider the blend of realism and fantasy Le Guin uses in this excerpt. The forest that the travelers pass through, where the trees grow in circles, is surely of another world, as is the "wotsit." But the travelers' plight of being lost in the woods is familiar, as is their persistence in moving forward in order to reach home.

FOR DISCUSSION AND REFLECTION

Discuss with students why fantasy writers need to include elements of realism in their stories.

➤ How would this excerpt from *The Eye of the Heron* be different without its realistic elements? (Without realistic elements, the story would be less believable and more difficult for readers to relate to and understand.)

➤ What are some techniques authors can use to help readers enter into and visualize the fantasy worlds they create? (Possible answers include: using sensory images, vivid description, strong details, and linking the fantasy elements with familiar, realistic ones.)

Writing

QUICK ASSESS

Do students' book covers:

✓ reflect time, thought, and creativity?

✓ depict their understandings of Le Guin's world?

Students are asked to create a cover for *The Eye of the Heron.* Their covers should reflect the view of the world Le Guin describes.

READING AND WRITING EXTENSIONS

➤ Ask students to think of a fantasy movie they've seen. Invite them to watch it again, this time looking for the various realistic elements of the movie. Then have students make a chart that compares the realistic and the fantastic elements. Have them present their charts to the class.

➤ Have students write a setting for their own science fiction or fantasy story. Remind them to include elements of realism as well as fantasy.

Two A Story in Ten Words

Critical Reading

FOCUS

Occasionally an imaginary object will be the central focus of a fantasy story. Ursula K. Le Guin developed one of her short stories around a "kerastion"—a musical instrument that has no sound.

BACKGROUND

Sometimes the most memorable part of a fantasy story will be its artifacts: its buildings, cars, weapons, and so on. In describing these inanimate objects, a fantasy writer often relies on "wishful thinking": what would I like to have, or what would my readers like to have?

➤ Ursula K. Le Guin invented a story to accompany a fantasy artifact that she found interesting. Although she knew her story would concern a musical instrument that has no sound and "is played only at a funeral," Le Guin knew she needed more. As a result, she wrote "The Kerastion" as a coming-of-age story that involves two memorable characters, Chumo and Kwatewa.

➤ In all fantasies, writers include fantasy artifacts that are not necessarily integral parts of the plot, but instead serve to set the stage—or the mood—for the fantasy world described. In "The Kerastion," Le Guin mentions artifacts such as "vauti-tuber," the "Body of Amajumo," and "Singing Sands." She never explains what these things are, but their presence helps create an "other worldly" feeling.

FOR DISCUSSION AND REFLECTION

Discuss with students what a fantasy story would be like without its fantastic artifacts.

➤ How would the mood of the story be different? (Without fantastic artifacts, the mood would be less fanciful and mysterious and more "down to earth.")

➤ How do fantastic artifacts add to the experience of reading fantasy? (Fantastic artifacts engage the reader's imagination and help draw the reader into the world of the story.)

Writing

QUICK ASSESS

Do students:

✓ clearly describe the object they've invented?

✓ introduce the fantasy artifact in their story openings?

✓ provide details of character, plot, or setting that support the artifact?

Students are asked to invent a fantasy artifact, describe it in a ten-word sentence, then begin a story in which the artifact appears.

READING AND WRITING EXTENSIONS

➤ Invite students to create a three-dimensional representation of a fantasy artifact they've read about in a work of science fiction or fantasy. Have them display the artifact they make along with a plot summary of the fantasy they read.

➤ Ask students to write a review of "The Kerastion" for the science fiction and fantasy section of their school's literary magazine. Their reviews should address these questions about Le Guin's work:

• Is she able to effectively balance realistic and fantastic elements in her story?

• Can readers easily connect with the characters and action she describes?

Three Truth in Fantasy

Critical Reading

"For the last fifty or sixty years, literature has been categorized as 'realism,' and if you weren't writing realism, you weren't respectable. I had to ignore that and say to myself that I could do things in science fiction that I could never do in realism."

BACKGROUND

In "Darkness Box," as in her other fantasies, Le Guin creates a careful balance of fantasy and reality. She uses both "fantasy artifacts" and "real" objects. Fantastic artifacts in the story include an alembic, a self-setting table, and a four-legged hut. Le Guin describes some of these artifacts in detail, and leaves others to the reader's imagination. Notice that there are also many "real" artifacts, including rabbit stew, onion-festooned rafters, and a boy's treasure shelf.

➤ She also describes both fantastic creatures and animals that are familiar. The sea serpent, the "familiar" that is treated as a member of the family, and the gryphon are all fantasy creatures. The horses on which the prince and his army ride and the whales that are hunted in the sea are realistic animals that appear in the story.

➤ Notice that Le Guin is also careful to combine both realism and fantasy when it comes to developing her characters. The clearest example of this is in the mother. At one point in the story she is quite lovely; at another point, she transforms herself into a crone.

FOR DISCUSSION AND REFLECTION

Discuss with students why it is so vital that readers be able to "step into" a fantasy writer's imaginary world.

➤ How do fantasy writers make their imaginary worlds engage the reader and seem "real"? (Possible answers include: they create characters that readers can connect with, include vivid descriptions of the imaginary world, and develop conflicts that have meaning both in the context of the story and in real life.)

➤ Why is it so important for a reader to be able to suspend disbelief? (Readers need to suspend disbelief so that they can become involved in the story and identify with the characters.)

Writing

QUICK ASSESS

Do students' answers:

✔ show careful thought?

✔ demonstrate an understanding of Le Guin's plot and characters?

✔ distinguish between fantastic and realistic elements in the story?

Students are asked to answer a series of questions about the realistic and fantastic aspects of Le Guin's story.

READING AND WRITING EXTENSIONS

➤ As an additional challenge, ask students to create a plot map for a fantasy story they'd like to write. Included on their maps should be a description of the artifacts, creatures, and characters they plan to use. Remind them about the need for realism in their stories.

➤ Have students read another work of science fiction or fantasy, and then write a book report about it to share with the class.

Four A Tissue of Lies

Critical Reading

FOCUS

Writers of fantasy draw on familiar concepts and objects in order to create their imaginary worlds. As a result, readers are able to connect the fantasy world to their own.

BACKGROUND

One of the ways a fantasy writer incorporates realism in a fantasy is by using items that have been "extrapolated" from the real world. Instead of inventing a completely imaginary object, fantasy writers often begin with a real object and give it fantastic characteristics.

➢ For example, think about the "wotsit" Lev holds in his hand in *The Eye of the Heron*. The wotsit, which clearly began as a toad, is a creature that has wings, three eyes, and a chameleon-like ability to change color to match its environment.

➢ In "The Kerastion," the musical instrument of the title is a flute, but it makes no sound, and is used only at funerals. In the world of Chumo and Kwatewa, a sand sculpture on the beach is a thing of beauty (as it is in the real world), but it is considered even more beautiful after the wind changes it into a "shapeless lump and feathering of white sand blown across the proving ground."

➢ Le Guin does the same sort of extrapolating in "Darkness Box" when she describes the beach scene with the sea serpent, "trackless" sand, and the bright sky that has no sun.

FOR DISCUSSION AND REFLECTION

Discuss with students why "extrapolation" is an effective technique for creating fantasy objects.

➢ Why might a fantasy writer choose to extrapolate rather than invent an object? (Readers can more readily identify with and understand stories that contain some familiar elements.)

➢ How does extrapolation affect a reader's interest in a story? (Extrapolation creates interest by making a story more believable and by helping readers connect the fantasy elements with their own experiences.)

Writing

QUICK ASSESS

Do students' paragraphs:

✓ describe the technique of extrapolation?

✓ list the elements they believe were extrapolated?

✓ describe the effectiveness of those elements?

Students will write a paragraph to explain how Le Guin extrapolated from the real world in one of her stories.

READING AND WRITING EXTENSIONS

➢ How is the technique of extrapolation used in Hollywood movies? Have students discuss examples of movies that contain extrapolated elements. Then ask them to "review" one of the movies. Their reviews should focus on whether or not the extrapolations were well done.

➢ Ask students to read a fantasy story written by another author in order to examine that author's use of extrapolation.

Five Dancing at the Edge of the World

Critical Reading

FOCUS

Ursula K. Le Guin on writing:

"…What artists do is make a particularly skillful selection of fragments of cosmos, unusually useful and entertaining bits chosen and arranged to give an illusion of coherence and duration amidst the uncontrollable streaming of events."

BACKGROUND

In this speech, Le Guin explains why she writes fantasy, and why the genre of fantasy holds so much appeal for her. She says that for her, fantasy is a way of discovering new worlds in a time when there are very few "real" worlds left to discover. Fantasy offers Le Guin a temporary escape from a world that has proven problematic—a Lost World—to a world that she can control and understand and revel in.

➤ In her speech, Le Guin makes it clear that although she chooses to describe imaginary worlds, she does not plan to ignore the problems of the real world. She intends to participate in the "dance of renewal, the dance that made the world [that] was always danced here at the edge of things, on the brink, on the foggy coast" of her beloved home.

➤ Le Guin also makes a point of explaining that the worlds she describes are not purely fantasy: "To make something is to invent it, to discover it is to uncover it, like Michaelangelo cutting away the marble that hid the statue." If you believe what Le Guin says, she may be describing worlds that already exist somewhere, or worlds that may exist sometime in the future.

FOR DISCUSSION AND REFLECTION

Discuss with students Le Guin's view of fantasy.

➤ According to Le Guin, why does fantasy appeal to so many people? (Fantasy allows the reader to escape to and become immersed in an alternative world.)

➤ How does Le Guin's feeling that we are "inhabitants of a Lost World" fuel her desire to write fantasy? (Through fantasy, Le Guin is able to explore new worlds that are coherent and complete.)

Writing

QUICK ASSESS

Do students' answers:

✔ reflect an understanding of Le Guin's purpose in writing?

✔ show they comprehend elements of fantasy?

✔ prove that they have thought carefully about Le Guin and her writing?

Students answer four questions about Le Guin's speech and then write a letter that explores Le Guin's work as a whole.

READING AND WRITING EXTENSIONS

➤ What does Le Guin have to say about using characters or ideas from other cultures? Do you agree that an author is justified in filching "an idea from China" or stealing "a god from India…"? Write a short position paper in which you explain your view.

➤ Imagine a conversation between Le Guin and one of the other authors you've read this year in class. What, for example, would Le Guin say to Sylvia Plath? What would Eve Merriam think about Le Guin? With a partner, write and perform a dialogue between Le Guin and another author.

Unit Overview

In "Essentials of Reading," students will explore five essentials of the reading process: making predictions, understanding the main idea, making inferences, rereading and reflecting, and examining the author's purpose. To help them think about each essential, students will read and respond to various types of literature: nonfiction, fiction, and poetry.

LITERATURE FOCUS

Lesson	Literature
1. Thinking With the Writer	**Rachel Carson**, "A Fable for Tomorrow" from *A Silent Spring* (Nonfiction)
2. Discovering the Main Idea	**Rachel Carson**, "Poisoned Water" from *A Silent Spring* (Nonfiction)
3. Reading Between the Lines	**David Guterson**, from *Snow Falling on Cedars* (Novel)
4. Doubling Back	
5. Author's Purpose	**Sylvia Plath**, "Sonnet" (Poetry) **Sylvia Plath**, letter to her mother (Letter)

READING FOCUS

1. Active readers examine the cause and effect of events in stories. Understanding why an event occurred engages them fully in the text.

2. The main idea—or theme—of a work is its underlying meaning. To find the main idea, first find the subject of the piece. The main idea is what the author has to say about the subject.

3. Drawing inferences about what you read will help you understand what the author is really saying. Each inference you make will bring you one step closer to the main idea.

4. Returning to a piece of writing for a second—and sometimes a third— reading increases your understanding of the meaning of the piece.

5. Identifying and understanding the writer's purpose adds to your understanding of what you read.

WRITING FOCUS

1. Write a paragraph that examines cause-and-effect relationships in a work of nonfiction.

2. Compare and contrast the main ideas of two essays by the same author.

3. Write a journalistic piece that describes and makes inferences about a character from a novel.

4. Write about how perceptions of a story change when additional background information is provided.

5. Explore author's purpose by examining a poem and a letter the author wrote about the poem.

One Thinking with the Writer

Critical Reading

FOCUS

From *A Silent Spring* by Rachel Carson: "Then a strange blight crept over the area and everything began to change. Some evil spell had settled on the community …."

Carson uses a tense, suspenseful, storytelling style to invite the reader to make predictions and look for cause and effect relationships.

BACKGROUND

Active readers repeatedly make predictions and look for cause-and-effect relationships as they read. Some writers encourage the use of these reading strategies through the tone, style, and structure of their writing. As they read this excerpt from *A Silent Spring*, students might ask themselves: what are some of the many ways Rachel Carson invites us to make predictions?

➤ In "A Fable for Tomorrow," Carson alternates short sentences with long ones and uses a great deal of imagery and figurative language. These techniques, both typical of oral storytelling, tend to grab and hold the reader's attention.

➤ Carson makes her dramatic announcement that ". . .every one of these disasters has actually happened somewhere, and many real communities have already suffered a substantial number of them," to shock the reader. She is shattering your predictions and, she hopes, your complacency about the environment.

FOR DISCUSSION AND REFLECTION

Discuss why making predictions as we read helps us engage with a text.

➤ What are some methods an author can use to encourage predictions? (Authors encourage prediction by building suspense, providing clues about outcomes, not revealing too much early on, and using foreshadowing.)

➤ How can making predictions affect or enhance the reading experience? (Predicting helps readers become engaged in and actively involved with the text.)

Writing

QUICK ASSESS

Do students' paragraphs:

✓ utilize information from their charts?

✓ explain what they think caused the problem?

✓ offer support for their ideas?

Students are asked to complete a cause and effect chart and then write a paragraph about what they think might have caused the "silent spring."

READING AND WRITING EXTENSIONS

➤ Ask students to find another essay that explores environmental problems and then compare and contrast its style to Carson's in "A Fable for Tomorrow." Which essay is more compelling? Why?

➤ Invite students to try writing a short story that encourages readers to make predictions about the action or the characters. Encourage them to use some of Carson's techniques.

Two Discovering the Main Idea

Critical Reading

FOCUS

Rachel Carson on pesticide use: "Unless we do bring these chemicals under better control, we are certainly headed for disaster."

The use of pesticides is the subject of Rachel Carson's "Poisoned Water." To find the main idea of a piece, look for the point the author wants to make about the subject.

BACKGROUND

Remind students that Carson's *A Silent Spring* was first published in 1962, at a time when the environment was not a major issue for the American public. Most people were familiar with DDT, and in fact used it often on their lawns and gardens. Imagine the shock readers must have felt when they discovered the cause for the silent spring Carson describes. By setting the reader up to feel this shock and dismay, Carson adds considerable drama to her main idea.

➤ It's not enough for a writer to merely state his or her main idea. The author must provide strong support and clarification so that readers can understand and accept the thesis. Sometimes an author will state his or her main idea right at the beginning of the piece. Other times, an author will build slowly toward the main idea, as Carson does. By the time Carson states her main idea in the second paragraph, she has already offered the reader several different pieces of support.

FOR DISCUSSION AND REFLECTION

Discuss with students the ways in which authors reveal and support the main idea.

➤ When does Carson reveal her main idea in "Poisoned Water"? How does she support her main idea? (She reveals her main idea in the first sentence of the second paragraph. She supports the main idea with anecdotes, examples, and facts.)

➤ Why might an author want to build slowly toward the main idea? (By building slowly toward the main idea, the author creates suspense and interest, which make the reader want to read on.)

➤ Why is it so important that the author support the main idea? (When an author supports the main idea, the piece is more persuasive, effective, and believable.)

Writing

QUICK ASSESS

Do students' paragraphs:

✓ identify the main idea of both essays?

✓ explain similarities and differences between the two?

Students are asked to write a paragraph in which they compare and contrast the main ideas of the two Carson essays. Before they begin writing, they'll identify the subject of each piece.

READING AND WRITING EXTENSIONS

➤ Have students do some online or library research about DDT or another pesticide. How is the pesticide used today? Why is it used? What are some benefits and drawbacks of the pesticide? When they've finished researching, students should prepare an oral report for the class.

➤ In a nonfiction picture book, the writer usually makes a direct statement of the main idea. Ask students to write and illustrate a nonfiction picture book about a topic that is important to them. Remind them that their main ideas should be clearly stated.

Three Reading Between the Lines

Critical Reading

FOCUS

From *Snow Falling on Cedars* by David Guterson: "The accused man, Kabuo Miyamoto, sat proudly upright with a rigid grace, his palms placed softly on the defendant's table—the posture of a man who has detached himself insofar as this is possible at his own trial."

In this excerpt, David Guterson's brief description of Miyamoto invites the reader to make inferences about this character's thoughts, feelings, and motivations.

BACKGROUND

All readers make inferences as they read, though they're not necessarily aware of doing it. An inference is any reasonable conclusion—correct or incorrect—that a reader can draw from the evidence provided in the text. To help students understand how and why they make inferences, invite them to read this short excerpt from David Guterson's award-winning novel *Snow Falling on Cedars*. The excerpt focuses on Kabuo Miyamoto, a Japanese American accused of killing a fisherman on a small, remote island near Puget Sound.

➤ Many of the inferences a reader might make about this excerpt concern character. From what Guterson says, we can conclude that Miyamoto is a proud man who is quietly defiant in the face of the islanders' accusations. Although he is most likely frightened, he refuses to let people see his fear. The reader might also infer that there is at least some reasonable doubt about the defendant's guilt. He is a fastidious man with an "imperial bearing" who appreciates the beauty of the cedars, the snow, and the windswept island shoreline. These are characteristics that are not usually associated with a murderer.

FOR DISCUSSION AND REFLECTION

Discuss with students the inferences they can make about the other characters in this scene.

➤ What inferences can students make about this community of islanders? (The islanders are a small, close-knit, church-going community; they are concerned about and involved in the trial proceedings.)

➤ What can students infer about the jury's point of view? (Students might infer that the jury is biased against the accused man because he is an "outsider" accused of killing their friend and neighbor.)

Writing

QUICK ASSESS

Do students' articles:

✓ use a journalistic tone or style?

✓ describe Kabuo's demeanor?

✓ use language appropriate to the content?

Students are asked to imagine they are journalists writing an article about accused murderer Kabuo Miyamoto. As a prewriting activity, students record information about Miyamoto.

READING AND WRITING EXTENSIONS

➤ Have students examine how juries are chosen for trials. Hold a classroom discussion on how bias can affect a jury's decision. Suggest they look at some famous cases, such as the Scottsboro boys' trials, the Scopes Monkey trial, and Korematsu vs. the United States.

➤ Invite students to think about other memorable courtroom scenes they have read about or seen in movies, such as the riveting courtroom scenes in *To Kill a Mockingbird* or *Presumed Innocent*. Have them offer a synopsis of "their" scene to the class.

Four Doubling Back

Critical Reading

FOCUS

On a first reading of *Snow Falling on Cedars,* readers may not notice the nuances of tone, style, and language that characterize Guterson's writing. "Enormous hills, soft green with cedars, rose and fell in every direction. The island homes were damp and moss covered and lay in solitary fields...."

A second or even third reading of a text can enhance appreciation and understanding of a writer's work.

BACKGROUND

The first time we read a work, we might take note of the subject or theme, but we often don't notice the ways in which the author develops that subject or theme. On a second reading, the reader, no longer distracted by the question of what might happen, can concentrate on elements of language, style, point of view, and so on. In "Doubling Back," students are asked to return to the Guterson excerpt and take note of what they missed on their first readings.

➤ On a second reading of the selection, students might begin to notice some specifics about Guterson's writing style. He takes the time to methodically describe everything he sees. Students might also notice his word choices, his imagery, and his use of sensory language. In discussing Guterson's language, for example, students might remark on his descriptions of the "humid, overbearing swelter" of heat, and the "smell of sour mildew."

➤ After their second readings, students will read the Guterson excerpt a third time, now privy to some additional knowledge about plot and character. How does this information change their understanding of Kabuo?

FOR DISCUSSION AND REFLECTION

Discuss with students how their perceptions of the work changed after rereading it.

➤ What figurative language does Guterson use? (Examples of figurative language include "sluggish radiators" and "furious, wind-whipped flakes.")

➤ What do students note about the author's bias? Is Guterson sympathetic toward Kabuo? (The words the author uses to describe Kabuo and the details he chooses to include suggest that Guterson is sympathetic to Kabuo.)

Writing

QUICK ASSESS

Do students' explanations:

✔ explain how and why their views changed as a result of the new information?

✔ use quotations from the text to support what they say?

Students are asked to explain how the knowledge they are given about the story affects their understanding of the action.

READING AND WRITING EXTENSIONS

➤ Have students construct a poem wholly from Guterson's language, picking up words and phrases to create a commentary on the excerpt from the novel.

➤ Now that students have read the excerpt three times, they should have an understanding of Guterson's use of poetic language. Have them write a poem that reflects this passage from *Snow Falling on Cedars.*

Five Author's Purpose

Critical Reading

When an author doesn't directly state his or her purpose for writing, it is the reader's job to infer the author's purpose from the language, tone, or theme of the work.

BACKGROUND

Most often an author will only hint at his or her purpose; it's up to the reader to string these hints together until intent is clear. This is the case with Sylvia Plath and her "Sonnet." According to "Sonnet," if you were to look inside a woman's head, you'd most likely see "scraps of rusted reverie . . . [and] notched tin platitudes concerning weather." Because of the poem's dark mood and violent imagery, we can infer that Plath's intention is to mourn the fate of women whose minds have been wasted, crushed by "steel palms of inclination."

➤ In a letter to her mother, Plath offers her purpose for writing the sonnet. She tells her mother that she wants to liken the mind to "a collection of mute mechanisms, trivial and smooth-functioning. . . ." Notice how the mind she describes in her sonnet cannot be reassembled once it is "cracked" open.

➤ The mood of Plath's sonnet is much darker than the mood she hints at in her letter. In the letter she makes the poem seem whimsical ("See what you can derive from this chaos. . . ."), when in fact the mood of her poem feels quite violent: ". . . take a skull and break it / The way you'd crack a clock. . . ."

FOR DISCUSSION AND REFLECTION

Discuss with students Plath's purpose in writing "Sonnet."

➤ How does the mood of the sonnet differ from the mood of the letter? (The poem is darker and more violent and depressing. The letter has a light, somewhat entertaining quality.)

➤ How does figuring out Plath's purpose in writing "Sonnet" enhance your reading of the poem? (Answers will vary but should focus on the link between the author's purpose and the poem's message or meaning.)

Writing

QUICK ASSESS

Can students:

✓ identify Plath's intent in the two pieces?

✓ explain whether the poem fulfills the intent she offers in her letter?

Students will decide if the poem fulfills the intent Plath offers in her letter.

READING AND WRITING EXTENSIONS

➤ Ask students to read some more of Plath's poetry (there is another poem on page 93 of the pupil's book). Is her mood always so dark? Invite students to write a short essay in which they analyze the mood of another Plath poem.

➤ Have students find a piece of expository nonfiction or a persuasive essay to examine in terms of author's purpose. Encourage them to write a paragraph or two about their findings.

Unit Overview

In "Story Landscapes," students are asked to explore the variety of landscapes, both physical and emotional, that are integral parts of any story. To help them in their explorations they will read and respond to works by Ray Bradbury, Gabriel García Márquez, Sandra Cisneros, and Robert Coover.

LITERATURE FOCUS

Lesson	Literature
1. Physical Landscapes in Story	**Ray Bradbury**, from "There Will Come Soft Rains" (Short Story) **Gabriel García Márquez**, from "Tuesday Siesta" (Short Story)
2. Emotional Landscapes in Story	**Sandra Cisneros**, "The Monkey Garden" from The House on Mango Street (Novel)
3. Changing Landscapes	
4. Exploring Your Own Landscapes	
5. Writing Your Landscapes	**Robert Coover**, from "The Magic Poker" (Short Story)

READING FOCUS

1. Writers use descriptions and details of setting to introduce a story's landscapes. These descriptions will often include information about the meaning and characters of the story.

2. Writers reveal what their characters are thinking and feeling by the way characters see and interpret the physical landscapes around them.

3. Writers often reveal characters' changing attitudes or reactions to situations by pointing out the differences in the way they describe the landscape around them.

4. Writers often look to places that hold special meaning for them for inspiration. Through these places, writers can explore their own feelings and ideas.

5. Capture landscapes from your own life stories in the same way that professional writers do. Then use them to help you write descriptions of physical and emotional landscapes, which help reveal your story's meaning.

WRITING FOCUS

1. Write two paragraphs—one that compares two settings and one that describes what setting can reveal about a story.

2. Create a map that explores a story's physical and emotional landscapes.

3. Write a new ending for a story.

4. Draw a map that explores the physical and emotional landscapes of a place important to you.

5. Write a description of the physical and emotional landscapes of your place.

One Physical Landscapes in Story

Critical Reading

FOCUS

From "There Will Come Soft Rains" by Ray Bradbury: *"Eight-one, tick-tock, eight-one o'clock, off to school, off to work, run, run, eight-one!"*

A talking clock echoing eerily through an empty house helps to set the mood and scene for this short story by Ray Bradbury.

BACKGROUND

"Physical Landscapes in Story" examines the function of a story's setting. In this lesson, students are shown examples of two very different settings and then asked to analyze each. In both cases, the setting is vital to the meaning of the story.

➤ In Ray Bradbury's "There Will Come Soft Rains," readers learn from the very first paragraph that the story takes place in the future at a time when clocks can talk and ovens can make breakfast without the help of human hands. Notice also how the futuristic objects that Bradbury includes in order to give us a sense of time also affect the mood of the story. The rhyme-calling appliances give the empty house an eerie feeling.

➤ The setting for García Márquez's "Tuesday Siesta" is a moving train. We learn that the story takes place in a tropical, though populated area (the train passes banana plantations and office buildings). The setting also reveals something about two of the passengers on the train: A mother and her daughter are grieving (they wear mourning clothes) and have little money (their clothes are "poor" and they travel in the third-class car).

FOR DISCUSSION AND REFLECTION

Discuss with students the various reasons a setting is important to a story.

➤ Why is it necessary for readers to be given a sense of time and place? (The physical setting locates the reader in the story.)

➤ What can a story's setting reveal about character? (Setting can be use to reveal characters' personalities, situations, thoughts, and feelings.)

➤ How are setting and mood related? (Setting can be used to set the mood of the story.)

Writing

QUICK ASSESS

Do students' comparisons:

✓ reflect an understanding of both settings?

✓ include a discussion of how setting can reveal information about meaning and characters?

Students are asked to compare the two settings. As prewriting activities, they'll analyze each setting separately.

READING AND WRITING EXTENSIONS

➤ Ask students to work together in small groups to create a children's book that explains what a setting is and the reasons it is important to a story. Students can add art if they like.

➤ Have students contribute to a "great settings in literature" bulletin board for their classroom. Ask each student to identify a setting from a book, poem, or story. Encourage them to draw pictures of the settings, and then explain briefly what makes each setting so memorable.

Two Emotional Landscapes in Story

Critical Reading

FOCUS

From "The Monkey Garden" by Sandra Cisneros: "We liked to think the garden could hide things for a thousand years. There beneath the roots of soggy flowers were the bones of murdered pirates and dinosaurs, the eye of a unicorn turned to coal."

Notice how the description of the garden reveals information not only about the setting, but also about the emotional life of the narrator.

BACKGROUND

In this lesson, students will explore how an author can reveal information about what a character is thinking and feeling by showing us how the character views the physical landscapes of the story. In Sandra Cisneros's "The Monkey Garden," for example, the reader can learn about the main character's feelings and attitudes through her description of the garden.

➤ Cisneros understands that character development is far more effective if it is done subtly. In "The Monkey Garden," she never comes right out and describes Esperanza, her main character.

➤ Instead, we are shown important aspects of Esperanza's personality through her descriptions of the landscape. For example, she is clearly disturbed by the kissing game the boys want to play in the garden. Through her reactions, we learn that she is resistant to change in any form, especially the changes that occur as one moves from childhood to adolescence.

FOR DISCUSSION AND REFLECTION

Discuss with students why the emotional landscape of a story can be as important as the physical landscape.

➤ What is the emotional landscape of a story? (The emotional landscape is the physical setting as filtered through the lens of one or more characters.)

➤ What can an emotional landscape reveal about character? (An emotional landscape can reveal what a character's attitudes, thoughts, and feelings are.)

➤ What techniques might an author use to create an emotional landscape? (One possible answer: An author can create an emotional landscape by having a character describe or interpret what is around him or her.)

Writing

QUICK ASSESS

Do students' maps:

✔ reflect both the physical and emotional aspects of the garden?

✔ demonstrate an understanding of the story's "emotional landscape"?

Students are asked to create a map of the garden and include symbols that represent Esperanza's feelings about particular places. As a prewriting activity, students will annotate the text.

READING AND WRITING EXTENSIONS

➤ Have students explore the emotional landscapes used in another type of writing. For example, students might explore how a copywriter establishes an emotional landscape for an ad. Have students explain their findings in an essay.

➤ Ask students to read another story by Cisneros, Bradbury, or García Márquez in order to compare and contrast it to the story in their daybooks. Their comparisons should focus on similarities and differences in setting.

Three Changing Landscapes

Critical Reading

FOCUS

From "The Monkey Garden" by Sandra Cisneros:"I looked at my feet in their white socks and ugly round shoes. They seemed far away. They didn't seem to be my feet anymore. And the garden that had been such a good place to play didn't seem mine either."

Characters' changing attitudes are often reflected in the way they view the landscapes around them.

BACKGROUND

Many times an author will make changes in a story's setting in order to indicate transitions or changes in theme, characters, or mood. In "The Monkey Garden," the main character notices changes in the garden at the same time she begins to see changes in herself. By the time the story ends, Esperanza's feelings about herself, her attitude toward others, and—significantly—her view of the garden, have all undergone radical transformations.

➤ Esperanza loves the monkey garden because it is a peaceful place, one in which she can allow her imagination to run wild. Almost as soon as the monkey leaves, however, Esperanza begins to notice changes in the garden which she finds disturbing. "Sleepy cars" soon clog the space, and weeds begin to sprout up. Although she's not happy about these changes, Esperanza tries to adjust. She learns to ignore the weeds and uses the rooftops of the cars for her games.

➤ What Esperanza can't adjust to are the changes she sees in herself: "Who was it that said I was getting too old to play the games? Who was it I didn't listen to?" She would rather play hide-and-seek among the cars than play kissing games with the boys. Eventually Esperanza understands that she'll have to accept the changes in herself and in her friends. When she reaches this understanding, however, her feelings about the monkey garden are changed forever.

FOR DISCUSSION AND REFLECTION

Discuss with students the mood of the story.

➤ What is the mood of the first part of the story? (Possible responses: carefree, relaxed, confident.)

➤ At what point does the mood change? In what ways does it change? (The mood changes when the narrator reveals that she tried to die in the garden; at this point the mood becomes tense and ominous.)

Writing

QUICK ASSESS

Do students' new endings:

✓ describe the garden through the eyes of Esperanza?

✓ reflect Esperanza's changed emotions?

Students are asked to write a new ending for the "The Monkey Garden."

READING AND WRITING EXTENSIONS

➤ Ask students to work with a partner to write a dialogue between Esperanza and Sally that explores their different reactions towards the incident in the garden. If they like, students can then dramatize their dialogues for the class.

➤ Invite students to write a journal entry about a time in their lives when they had to face up to changes in themselves, their friends, or their surroundings.

Four Exploring Your Own Landscapes

Critical Reading

FOCUS

Sandra Cisneros is a writer who writes what she knows. Although born in Chicago in 1954, Cisneros's language and style often span cultures and continents. She finds strength from her roots in the barrio, and is above all else determined to write unflinchingly about her world.

BACKGROUND

Most writers enjoy reflecting on how they get the ideas for their stories. The majority say their ideas come from their own experiences—the people they've met, the places they've visited, and the things they've seen. In this lesson, students are invited to consider how their own personal landscapes can provide material for interesting, engaging stories.

➤ As almost any writer will tell you, the most successful writers write what they *know*. They use the people they know best as models for their characters and the places they know best as models for their settings.

➤ Before they begin work on this lesson, students should stop for a moment and think about the people and places they know best. What place would they find easiest to describe? What person would they most want to write about? What time period do they find most interesting? Have them make some notes before they move on to the writing activity.

FOR DISCUSSION AND REFLECTION

Discuss with students how to create interesting landscapes for their readers.

➤ Why is it important for writers to offer readers plenty of detail when writing about setting? (Responses should focus on the importance of readers being able to visualize the place and time.)

➤ What are some examples of details Cisneros includes in "The Monkey Garden"? (Answers will vary.)

➤ How do these details help make the story interesting? (Details make the garden come alive and the story seem real.)

Writing

QUICK ASSESS

Do students' maps:

✔ show they understand the differences between "physical" and "emotional" landscapes?

✔ include notations about objects, places, and memorable events?

Students are asked to draw a map of a place that is important to them. They'll also note on their maps specific objects, places of interest, and events.

READING AND WRITING EXTENSIONS

➤ Tell students to imagine they've been invited to submit a "personal landscape" article to a teen magazine. They are free to write about any subject they choose, but they need to establish both a physical and an emotional landscape for their story.

➤ Have each student write a "mighty minute" presentation that explores his or her favorite place in their world. Remind students that they have only one minute to describe this place, so they will need to include only the most important details.

Five Writing Your Landscapes

Critical Reading

FOCUS

In "The Magic Poker," Robert Coover takes what could be an enticing setting—a secluded island—and manipulates details in order to make the setting sinister and imposing: "I deposit shadows and dampness, spin webs, and scatter ruins …I impose a hot midday silence, a profound and heavy stillness."

BACKGROUND

In this lesson, students learn that a writer can manipulate the details of a landscape in order to emphasize certain aspects of mood, theme, and characters. In his short story "The Magic Poker," Robert Coover takes advantage of this license by presenting to the reader a landscape that—in the hands of a different writer—might be calm, peaceful, and inviting.

➤ Think for a moment how Coover might have described the island in his story. This island *might have been* a secluded paradise. The bay *might have been* placid, and the depth *might have been* just perfect for swimming. Instead Coover describes an island that is abandoned, gray, and in ruins. By showing his readers only the ugliness of this island, Coover is able to establish a mood of unpleasantness, violence, and fear.

➤ Coover's description of the physical landscape also gives us clues about the emotional landscape of the person who "[wanders] the island, inventing it." It's clear that there is something wrong. The narrator hears the motor of an approaching boat as a "harsh snarl." And when he sees that the boat has two passengers aboard, what comes to mind first is the rusty poker.

FOR DISCUSSION AND REFLECTION

Discuss with students the various "landscapes" of this story.

➤ What does the reader learn about the physical landscape? (The physical landscape—the island—is neglected, abandoned, and unappealing.)

➤ In what ways is the physical landscape tied to the emotional landscape? (The physical landscape reflects the narrator's emotional landscape—bleak, unstable, and perhaps dangerous.)

Writing

QUICK ASSESS

Do students' paragraphs:

✓ clearly and precisely describe the place?

✓ use figurative language, sensory images, and strong details to add vitality to their writing?

Students are asked to write a description of a place on their maps. Remind them to include details that reflect the physical and emotional landscapes of the place they're describing.

READING AND WRITING EXTENSIONS

➤ In what ways does a movie director manipulate a landscape? What are some of the reasons a director would want to manipulate a movie's landscape? Students can write an essay in which they discuss Hollywood "landscape manipulation" or memorable landscapes in films.

➤ As a class, write the rest of Coover's story. Have small groups contribute paragraphs. Be sure that students keep Coover's writing style in mind and his tendency to manipulate settings in order to set the mood and heighten interest.

Unit Overview

In "Characters in Stories," students are invited to explore the many different ways authors have of creating memorable characters. By reading two excerpts from Margaret Atwood's *Cat's Eye,* and an excerpt from Tobias Wolff's autobiography, *This Boy's Life,* students can begin to see how writers use physical description, personality, behavior, and dialogue to create complex and memorable characters.

LITERATURE FOCUS

Lesson	Literature
1. Distinguishing Characteristics	**Margaret Atwood**, from *Cat's Eye* (Novel)
2. Character Motivation	
3. Character Development	**Margaret Atwood**, from *Cat's Eye* (Novel)
4. Point of View	
5. Dialogue Reveals Character	**Tobias Wolff**, from *This Boy's Life* (Autobiography)

READING FOCUS

1. A reader needs to determine the qualities that define a character and explain how each character contributes to the whole of the story.

2. Knowing what motivates characters helps you explain why they act the way they do.

3. Authors use various methods to show character development because in fiction, as in life, people are affected or changed by their experiences.

4. Point of view affects what is included in a story and how it is told.

5. The dialogue in a story reveals information about characters' motivations, values, and actions.

WRITING FOCUS

1. Write a character sketch, which describes a person by their qualities of character and actions, as well as physical appearance.

2. Write an imagined monologue, which will explain the motivations of a character in the story.

3. Analyze character development, explaining any change and its cause and importance.

4. Rewrite a scene from another point of view.

5. Write a dialogue between three characters you have created.

One Distinguishing Characteristics

Critical Reading

FOCUS

Margaret Atwood on fiction writing:

"It's the business of fiction writers to be plausible. That's another way of saying it's the business of the fiction writer to tell you lies you will believe!"

BACKGROUND

This lesson examines the ways authors create memorable characters. The excerpt from Margaret Atwood's *Cat's Eye* provides an excellent example. From the first sentence about Cordelia in paragraph three, Atwood deftly begins to bring her to life.

➤ "It's one of her friendly days" lets the reader know with no real description or even example, that this Cordelia is not always nice; there are some dark, rough edges around her. It foreshadows the incident at the bridge and helps make Cordelia's actions seem in keeping with her character. Atwood tells us that Cordelia can be mean, so it's really no surprise when she is.

➤ Atwood does an equally convincing job with the remaining characters. Note how in the seventh paragraph, Atwood provides important insights into Elaine's character just from Elaine's comment that "For once she [Grace] is the one left behind." This not only adds to our understanding of Elaine but, again, helps set up the powerful episode to come.

➤ Atwood manages to tell us much about her characters without actually describing them physically. She lets their actions (and Elaine's inner thoughts) speak for themselves.

FOR DISCUSSION AND REFLECTION

Discuss with students why realistic, interesting characters are important to stories.

➤ How can readers use details about characters to better understand a story? (Readers can use details to make inferences about a character's motives and characteristics.)

➤ What techniques can writers use to bring their characters to life? (Possible responses: physical details, dialogue, actions, other characters' commentary, etc.)

Writing

QUICK ASSESS

Does the character sketch:

✓ include enough details to bring the character to life?

✓ go beyond physical description?

✓ show an understanding of Atwood's techniques?

Students will use some of Atwood's techniques to write brief character sketches. As a prewriting activity, they will brainstorm distinguishing features about their characters and organize them into a cluster diagram. Encourage students to move beyond using physical details alone to describe their characters. Have them refer back to the excerpt and model their own sketches on Atwood's techniques.

READING AND WRITING EXTENSIONS

➤ As an additional challenge, have students leave out all physical description from their sketches. Can they provide enough details about their characters through other means?

➤ Have students work in pairs to write and present a dialogue between their two characters. Encourage them to bring their characters to life through their words and actions.

Two Character Motivation

Critical Reading

FOCUS

An important aspect of character analysis is character motivation. Writers assume the reader will infer why a character acts in a particular way or says a particular thing. Analyzing character motivation is an essential part of reading.

BACKGROUND

Margaret Atwood's *Cat's Eye* is the story of painter Elaine Risley, who returns to her hometown for a retrospective of her work. She has been away for more than 30 years and as she wanders the streets of her city, Risley is assaulted with the "tyrannical and obsessive memories" of her life there. No longer able to ignore the past, she is forced to come to terms with her feelings about a group of girls she called friends, but who proved to be her worst tormentors.

➤ Atwood gives us several clues about what motivates Cordelia to act the way she does. For example, we know that she can be mean-spirited ("Her face is hard again, her eyes baleful") and controlling ("She likes everything she does to be done on purpose"). We also know that it's possible that she taunts Elaine because it has become a habit, one that she doesn't plan to break: "Maybe she's gone too far, hit, finally, some core of resistance in [Elaine]."

➤ Atwood also gives several clues about what motivates Elaine to agree to go into the ravine. She is obviously a timid and self-conscious girl who is not used to feeling completely exhilarated or completely happy. The reader knows that Elaine is afraid. It's because of her fear of consequences—what her parents might do if she tells, what Cordelia might do if she refuses, what the other girls might think if she resists—that Elaine decides to go into the ravine to retrieve her hat.

FOR DISCUSSION AND REFLECTION

Discuss with students what they think motivates the other girls in the group to side with Cordelia.

➤ How do the girls act toward Cordelia before she falls in the snow? How do they act after she falls? (They are all happy and friendly before Cordelia falls. Afterward, Elaine, Grace, and Carol are afraid. Grace and Carol are relieved to be able to side with Cordelia against Elaine.)

➤ What is these girls' attitude toward Elaine? How do they show their feelings? (Answers will vary, but most students will say that they are mean and unfair to Elaine.)

Writing

QUICK ASSESS

Do students' monologues:

✓ maintain the point of view?

✓ reveal character's motivation?

Students are asked to write monologues in which they explore Cordelia's or Grace's actions during the incident with Elaine. As a prewriting activity, they will explore character motivation for Cordelia, Elaine, Grace, and Carol.

READING AND WRITING EXTENSIONS

➤ As an additional challenge, have each student write another monologue, this time from the point of view of a different character. Their monologues should offer some clues about character motivation.

➤ Have students write a prediction of what they think might happen next in the story. What will Elaine do? What will the other girls do?

Three Character Development

Critical Reading

FOCUS

From *Cat's Eye* by Margaret Atwood: "I no longer feel the sinking in my gut . . . ."

Characters develop throughout a story, and it is important to identify the key incidents that shape the character's attitudes and perceptions.

BACKGROUND

In literature there are essentially two types of characters: *flat* characters and *round* characters. A flat character lacks complexity and has no capacity for development or change. A round character is complex and often (but not always) undergoes a change during the course of the story.

➤ Many times a character must experience a crisis before change—or character development—is possible. In *Cat's Eye*, the crisis is Elaine's fall into the water, and her experience of delerium afterward. Notice how at the point that she falls into the stream, she is a girl unable to exert control over her life. She allows herself to be ordered around by a cold-hearted, unkind bully who is completely indifferent to other people's feelings. After her brush with death, Elaine no longer cares if Cordelia and the other girls approve of her: "I am still a coward, still fearful; none of that has changed. But I turn and walk away from her. . . ." Because she has nearly died—and because she managed to save herself without the help of her "friends"—Elaine begins to understand that she doesn't need to rely on others to make her feel safe and happy. For the very first time she understands what these girls are: "I can see the greed in their eyes. It's as if I can see right into them. Why was I unable to do this before?"

FOR DISCUSSION AND REFLECTION

Discuss with students the causes for the change in Elaine's character.

➤ How does Elaine's fall through the ice change her feelings about the three girls? (She begins to see them and their actions toward her for what they are.)

➤ How does Elaine's fall through the ice change her feelings about herself? (Responses will vary, but should center around the idea that by surviving this incident Elaine discovers some of her own strength of character.)

Writing

QUICK ASSESS

Do students' paragraphs:

✔ explain the changes in Elaine's character and what caused them?

✔ support their interpretations with evidence from the text?

Students will write three paragraphs in which they explore changes in Elaine's character. As a prewriting activity, they will work on a before and after chart that shows how Elaine changes as a result of the ravine incident.

READING AND WRITING EXTENSIONS

➤ Ask students to write a short essay about a time they experienced a "crisis" that changed the way they viewed the world. What was the crisis? Why did it affect them so profoundly?

➤ Ask students to create a "Before and After" chart that traces character development in another story they've read. Before they make their charts, have them write a one-paragraph summary of the plot.

Four **Point of View**

C r i t i c a l   R e a d i n g

FOCUS

From *Cat's Eye* by Margaret Atwood: "I can see the greed in their eyes. It's as if I can see right into them."

Point of view is the vantage point from which a story is presented. It is *who* tells the story and *how* it is told.

BACKGROUND

Margaret Atwood's attitude toward point of view: "You will always have partial points of view, and you'll always have the story behind the story that hasn't come out yet." Why is it important to understand the author's point of view? Why does it matter who tells the story? In this lesson, students will return again to the two *Cat's Eye* excerpts and reflect on the role the narrator—Elaine—plays in the story.

➤ Because Elaine is the narrator of the story, we see only her perspective on the events. When she implies that Cordelia is cruel and Grace is a fool, we have to take her word for it. When she tells us that the girls left the bridge on purpose—in order to make her pay for her laughter—we again have to believe that she is correct in what she says. Elaine's perspective becomes the reader's perspective, then, and we find ourselves siding with her throughout.

➤ Consider how *Cat's Eye* would change if the story were told from the point of view of another character—Cordelia, for example. Lines like "It's one of her friendly days" and "For a moment she looks like someone I don't know, a stranger, shining with unknown, good possibilities" would not be included. If Cordelia were the narrator, we'd have a much clearer view of what motivates her to behave the way she does, and it's quite possible that we'd feel much more sympathetic toward her.

FOR DISCUSSION AND REFLECTION

Ask students to discuss point of view as a literary technique.

➤ How does first-person point of view differ from third-person point of view? What are the advantages and disadvantages of each? (Answers will vary, but should focus on the subjective nature of a first-person narrator versus the more objective voice of a third-person one.)

➤ What is the effect if the narrator is *third-person omniscient?* (A third-person omniscient narrator has access to the thoughts and actions of all the characters and so is able to give a full picture of all their points of view.)

W r i t i n g

QUICK ASSESS

Does students' writing:

✔ demonstrate an ability to maintain a single point of view?

✔ show how a change in point of view can change the story?

Students are asked to rewrite the incident in the story from the point of view of one of the other characters. When they finish, they explain how the point of view they offer changes the story.

READING AND WRITING EXTENSIONS

➤ Ask students to rewrite the incident on the bridge using a *third-person omniscient* point of view. Explain that in this point of view the narrator stands outside the story as an observer and is able to see into the minds of all the characters.

➤ Have students imagine they are Elaine and write the journal entry she might have written on the day she walked away from Cordelia and the other two girls. Remind them to maintain Elaine's point of view throughout the entry.

Five Dialogue Reveals Character

Critical Reading

FOCUS

Another way an author can reveal information about character is through what the characters *say*. A story's dialogue often tells us quite a bit about character motivation, character development, and character emotions.

BACKGROUND

In order to explore the ways dialogue can provide information to the reader, students will read an excerpt from Tobias Wolff's autobiography.

➤ Judging from what they say to each other and to young Tobias, Sister James and the priest are both kind-hearted, though a bit naive. In order to encourage Tobias to open up to the priest, Sister James confesses two or three childhood sins. Instead of inspiring Tobias to reveal his sins, he uses her sins as his confession.

➤ The reader also knows from early on that the priest is kindhearted. He offers a fatherly solution ("Needs to relax. Nothing like a glass of milk for that") when Tobias is "unable" to confess his sins. When Tobias does make his "confession," the priest seems taken aback, but doesn't challenge the confession.

➤ Interestingly, though he has less to say than the other two characters, we are still able to form some opinions of Tobias. We learn from this scene that he knows when to keep his mouth shut and let others do the talking. We also know from the respectful way he speaks and acts that he's not interested in offending anyone, he just does not know what he's supposed to say.

FOR DISCUSSION AND REFLECTION

Discuss with students why well-written dialogue is important to a story.

➤ What are some characteristics of effective dialogue? (Responses will vary.)

➤ How can readers use dialogue to better understand character and theme? (Readers can use dialogue to infer many unsaid things about a character's background, attitudes, and actions.)

Writing

QUICK ASSESS

Is the student's dialogue:

✓ engaging?

✓ well-written?

✓ enlightening in terms of character?

Students are asked to write a dialogue between three characters of their own creation. As a prewriting exercise, they will make a cluster chart that explores some distinguishing traits for the three characters.

READING AND WRITING EXTENSIONS

➤ Ask students to create a continuation of Wolff's story by writing the conversation that takes place between Tobias and Sister James after he leaves the confessional for a second time.

➤ Have students examine another piece of literature to see the ways in which another author creates effective dialogue. Is this author's technique similar to Wolff's? In what ways? Does the author use more or less dialogue?

SHIFTING FORMS

Unit Overview

In "Shifting Forms: Nonfiction and Poetry," students will compare and contrast several different aspects of nonfiction and poetry. Throughout the unit they'll be encouraged to watch for the ways our perspectives or attitudes toward an event change when the structure or form of the writing changes.

LITERATURE FOCUS

Lesson	Literature
1. Reading Nonfiction	**Jane E. Brody**, from "Many Smokers Who Can't Quit Are Mentally Ill" (Nonfiction)
2. Creating an Impression	**Luis J. Rodriguez**, from *Always Running* (Autobiography)
3. Shifting Emphasis	**Luis J. Rodriguez**, from *Always Running* (Autobiography)
4. Shifting Genres	**Luis J. Rodriguez**, " 'Race' Politics" (Poetry)
5. Comparing Genres	

READING FOCUS

1. Critical reading of nonfiction requires evaluating the objectivity of the selection.
2. Authors often use repeated details and a series of similar events to create a strong impression in the reader's mind.
3. Authors can change the reader's impressions of people and events through the details they choose to present.
4. Different genres can provide a different focus for an event.
5. Details often assume different meanings in different forms. They may be subjective or objective, depending on the writer's involvement in the events and the impression he or she wants to create.

WRITING FOCUS

1. Rewrite a newspaper article as a persuasive letter and then compare the two writing forms.
2. Write down impressions of characters and reflect on how a narrative changes when point of view changes.
3. Explore how your impressions of characters change over the course of a story.
4. Write about how a change in genre can affect the reader's perceptions of characters and events.
5. Rewrite an autobiographical excerpt as a poem.

One Reading Nonfiction

C r i t i c a l   R e a d i n g

FOCUS

How factual or objective a work of nonfiction is depends on the type of nonfiction and the writer's position or bias. When reading nonfiction, it is important to evaluate the writer's points and the objectivity of the selection.

BACKGROUND

An important part of reading nonfiction is understanding that no writing can be completely unbiased; there is a certain degree of subjectivity in any piece. However, certain kinds of nonfiction are by their nature more objective than others. For example, we expect a scientific report to be more objective than an autobiography. In this lesson, students will explore what constitutes objectivity in nonfiction by examining an article from the *New York Times*.

➤ Two of the most important questions a reader can ask about a nonfiction piece are "What is the thesis statement?" and "How well does the author explain, develop, and support the thesis?" In a newspaper article, the thesis almost always appears in the article's lead, as it does in Jane Brody's piece. In fact, her thesis is her first sentence: "People who have been smoking for years . . . have more health problems than either they or their physicians realize."

➤ Brody uses the body of the article to develop and support her thesis. Notice how she offers her strongest piece of support right away, in the second paragraph. She quotes a scientist—someone a reader would probably consider objective—who says that smokers are at risk for "major depressive orders, adult attention deficit hyperactivity disorder," and so on. Throughout the article, Brody offers questions and research to support her points.

FOR DISCUSSION AND REFLECTION

Discuss with students the objectivity of Brody's article.

➤ Does Brody offer facts, opinions, or both? Explain. (Brody offers facts in the form of conclusions based on research. She also includes opinions, "This not-too-surprising conclusion . . .")

➤ Would you say she is completely objective? Why or why not? (Brody is not completely objective because she interprets the facts and presents only one side of the issue.)

W r i t i n g

QUICK ASSESS

Do students:

✓ succeed in changing Brody's article into a persuasive letter?

✓ offer support for the claims they make in the letter?

Students are asked to rewrite the newspaper article as a persuasive letter. As a prewriting activity, students will discuss with a partner the objectivity vs. subjectivity of Brody's article.

READING AND WRITING EXTENSIONS

➤ Ask students to make an "objectivity" vs. "subjectivity" scrapbook out of newspaper and magazine articles. Have them include with each article an explanation of why they think the article is subjective or objective.

➤ Have students spend a week acting as "roving reporters." Their assignment: to write an objective article about an event they witness during the week.

Two Creating an Impression

Critical Reading

FOCUS

Luis J. Rodriguez, describing his brother: "He also took delight in seeing me writhe in pain, cry or cower, vulnerable to his own inflated sense of power."

In his autobiography, Rodriguez selects a series of details and events that succeed in creating a strong impression of his older brother.

BACKGROUND

For the most part, readers do not expect objectivity from an autobiography. A writer of an autobiography manipulates details and facts in order to create a specific impression on the reader. In this lesson, students will read an excerpt from Luis J. Rodriguez's autobiography, *Always Running*, and then think about the impression Rodriguez creates with his writing.

➤ Rodriguez clearly intends to leave the reader with a strong impression of what his childhood was like. To that end he spares no details about his life in Watts, no matter how disturbing. Because he uses so many sensory details (the smell of the weeds, the "scrape" of the branches on the window, and so on), he succeeds in making the reader feel a part of all that he describes.

➤ Rodriguez also uses sensory details to give readers a strong impression of what his brother was like as a child. Rano was often "wracked with a scream which he never let out" and his face was "dark with meanness." Although we know Luis's view of Rano is not exactly objective—we only see Luis's side of the story—the reader is quickly convinced that Luis was tormented by his older brother.

FOR DISCUSSION AND REFLECTION

Discuss with students why this excerpt is an example of subjective nonfiction.

➤ Why is this piece an example of nonfiction? (It is nonfiction because it depicts real situations and events from Luis Rodriguez's childhood.)

➤ In what ways is this piece of nonfiction subjective? (The piece is subjective in that the author selects and emphasizes certain details to create an effect; he interprets events: ". . . I remember my brother as the most dangerous person alive"; and he presents only one point of view—his own.)

Writing

QUICK ASSESS

Do students' answers:

✓ describe their impressions of both Luis and Rano?

✓ show they understand how a change in point of view can change a reader's impression of the story?

Students are first asked to reflect on their impressions of Luis and Rano. They are then asked to write a paragraph examining how the same incidents would be portrayed in Rano's biography.

READING AND WRITING EXTENSIONS

➤ Encourage students to reread the parts of the excerpt that describe Luis's and Rano's mother. Ask students to rewrite an incident from the excerpt from the point of view of the boys' mother. How does her point of view change the story?

➤ Invite students to describe an event that had a profound effect on them as a child. Why was the event so significant? What happened? How did they react?

Three Shifting Emphasis

Critical Reading

FOCUS

In another excerpt from his autobiography, Rodriguez paints a more sympathetic portrait of his brother Rano. As a result, the reader's impression of Rano changes.

"Up until then my brother had never shown any emotion to me other than disdain . …But for this once he looked at me, tears welled in his eyes, blood streamed from several cuts—lips and cheeks swollen."

BACKGROUND

For this lesson, students are asked to read another excerpt from *Always Running*. In this part of his autobiography, Rodriguez describes how he and his brother crossed over to the "Anglo" section of town to buy groceries. While there, a group of white boys brutally beat Rano. Because of the way Rodriguez describes the incident, the reader's impression of Rano (and Luis) changes. Encourage students to keep notes on how their perspectives of the two boys change while reading the excerpt.

➤ By the time the white boys finish, Rano is bleeding and barely able to walk. The Rano we met in the previous excerpt—the brutal monster who takes pleasure in pain—has turned into a suffering young boy frightened that others will find out he has cried. For the first time the reader can sympathize with Rano.

➤ Because of the beating, the relationship between the two boys undergoes a subtle shift. Although Rano is still in charge, he is forced to ask a favor of his brother— something he has never had to do before. And even though Luis feels compassion for his brother, he can't help himself from taking a quiet pleasure in the change in their relationship.

FOR DISCUSSION AND REFLECTION

Discuss with students how their impressions of Rano have changed.

➤ In what ways is the author's viewpoint different in this excerpt? (The author is more sympathetic to Rano in this excerpt.)

➤ How does the change in the author's viewpoint affect students' feelings about Rano? (Students are likely to feel pity for Rano and find him more likable and appealing than they did previously.)

Writing

QUICK ASSESS

Do students' explanations:

✓ explore the ways their impressions have changed?

✓ explain the reasons for this change?

Students write about their impressions of Luis and Rano and how their impressions of each character have changed.

READING AND WRITING EXTENSIONS

➤ Ask students to write a paragraph in which they explore a relationship that is important to them. Remind them to use sensory language and plenty of details in their writing.

➤ Have students imagine a scenario in which Luis and Rano encounter two children from the Anglo neighborhood who have crossed the tracks into Watts. Given the boys' experience buying groceries in South Gate, how might they react? Have students write a paragraph describing what Luis and Rano say and do in this situation.

Four Shifting Genres

Critical Reading

FOCUS

A change in genre can change the focus of the events described. If a writer switches from short story to essay, for example, the tone, the mood, the underlying meaning, and even the effect on the reader can change radically.

BACKGROUND

Lesson Four gives students the opportunity to see how a shift in genre can provide a different focus for an event. Students are invited to read another version of Luis's experience in the Anglo section of town. In this retelling of the story, Luis uses verse rather than prose. As they read " 'Race' Politics," students should note any differences in tone and mood they find. Is one piece angrier than the other? Which piece do students find easier to relate to? Why?

➤ Although there are many differences between the poem and the autobiographical excerpt, the most striking difference lies in the tone of the two pieces. Notice that in the poem, Rodriguez is angry—far angrier than he seems in his autobiography. In the poem he shows his fury in nearly every line. He tells of his sense of "powerlessness," and the "narrow line of hate" that separates the Hispanics from the whites; he talks about how Rano was punched "until swollen and dark blue" and how the white boys "threw us back, / dirty and lacerated, / back to Watts. . . ." It's as if all the emotions he forced himself to suppress when telling the story in his autobiography erupt when he decides to write his poem.

FOR DISCUSSION AND REFLECTION

Discuss with students how Rodriguez changes his focus in the poem "'Race' Politics."

➤ Is Rodriguez more objective in his autobiographical excerpt or his poem? (The poem is less objective and focuses more on feelings and emotions.)

➤ Why do you think Rodriguez chose to vent his feelings in his poem rather than in his autobiography? (Answers should focus on the idea that autobiography is a nonfictional form that draws on facts, while poetry is more subjective and emotional.)

Writing

QUICK ASSESS

Do students' paragraphs:

✓ explore their impressions of Rano in the poem?

✓ compare their own reactions to the two Rodriguez pieces?

Students are asked to describe how their reactions to the beating incident changed when the writer changed genres.

READING AND WRITING EXTENSIONS

➤ Ask students to look through their own writing and choose one piece they'd like to rewrite in a new genre. They might convert a story into a poem, for example, or an essay into a short story.

➤ Ask students to write a poem about a significant event in their lives. They can use any structure they like for their poems, though they should feel free to model their writing style on Rodriguez's " 'Race' Politics."

Five Comparing Genres

Critical Reading

FOCUS

Writers interpret and represent details differently when writing in different genres.

BACKGROUND

In this lesson, students are asked to compare Rodriguez's poem about the beating to his autobiographical recollection of the same event. It should become clear to students when they compare the two selections that a set of details in a piece of writing can assume a completely different meaning when the structure or genre of the writing changes.

➤ Notice how Rodriguez uses many of the same details in both the poetry and the prose. For example, the torn-up sofa and discarded grocery carts appear in both works, as do the soup cans, bread, and candy. The walk to the grocery store is essentially the same, and so is the first moment of the attack. The fight itself and the injuries the boys sustain are also very similar.

➤ The way in which Rodriguez presents these details in the two works is very different, however. Rodriguez is much more matter-of-fact in his autobiography. In the poem, Rodriguez allows his emotions to come through. He wants his readers to feel the fury and powerlessness he felt during the attack. By using fierce language ("a line of power"), loaded images ("those lines that crisscross / the abdomen of this land"), and biting sarcasm ("Oh, this was plenty reason / to hate us"), Rodriguez shows readers his anger and encourages us to be angry too.

FOR DISCUSSION AND REFLECTION

Ask students to compare Rodriguez's poem to the excerpt from his autobiography.

➤ What similarities and differences are there between the two selections? Explain. (Many details are the same in both pieces; the author's tone and reaction to the details are different.)

➤ Which selection makes a stronger impression on the reader? Why? (Many students will cite the poetry selection because of its strong emotional impact.)

Writing

QUICK ASSESS

Do students' poems:

✓ use the excerpt from Lesson Two as the basis for their verse?

✓ convey impressions of the two characters?

✓ reflect time, effort, and creativity?

Students are asked to turn the Rodriguez excerpt from Lesson Two into a poem. As a prewriting activity, they'll fill in a chart that compares Rodriguez's prose to his poem.

READING AND WRITING EXTENSIONS

➤ Have students imagine they are Luis as an adult. Luis wants to explain to his son or daughter what happened to him when he was six. Ask students to write what they think Luis might want to tell the child. Remind them to pay particular attention to tone.

➤ As an additional challenge, ask students to examine the poems they wrote for this lesson. What impression did they want to create? What details did they include to help them create that impression? Have students explain their poems in a paragraph.

Unit Overview

Because no two poems are exactly alike, readers need to have at hand several different strategies that can be used to help them understand the style, structure, and theme of a poem. In "Interpretations: A New Look at Poems," students will practice using four different strategies to help them interpret poetry by E. E. Cummings, Walt Whitman, Marylita Altaha, and Langston Hughes.

LITERATURE FOCUS

Lesson	Literature
1. Getting a Sense of a Poem	**E. E. Cummings**, "if everything happens that can't be done" (Poetry)
2. Making Sense	
3. Juxtaposing Texts	**Walt Whitman**, "When I Heard the Learn'd Astronomer" (Poetry) **Marylita Altaha**, "Have You Ever Hurt About Baskets?" (Poetry)
4. Using Venn Diagrams	
5. Selecting Strategies	**E. E. Cummings**, "R-P-O-P-H-E-S-S-A-G-R" (Poetry) **Langston Hughes**, "The Negro Speaks of Rivers" (Poetry)

READING FOCUS

1. Get an impression of what a poem means before trying to interpret it.
2. Respond to the questions and comments of others to help make sense of a poem.
3. Juxtaposing texts gives you different perspectives on a topic. Use those perspectives to interpret each poem.
4. Comparing and contrasting helps you determine a poet's point of view toward the topic.
5. Being aware of how you read poems and of the various interpretive strategies available to you will help you read poetry.

WRITING FOCUS

1. Write down impressions of and a question about the poem.
2. Describe what you think the poem is about.
3. Explore the connections between two poems by examining elements such as subject and tone.
4. Compare and contrast three poems to determine each poet's point of view.
5. Write an interpretive summary of a poem and analyze the strategies you used to get at the poem's meaning.

One Getting a Sense of a Poem

Critical Reading

FOCUS

Most poems need to be read more than once. On a first reading, the reader forms a general impression. A second or third reading often provides a perspective for interpreting or understanding the poem.

BACKGROUND

Why do many people find poetry so difficult to enjoy? Usually it's because they feel they don't understand it—the form is confusing or the meaning is not clear. In this lesson, students will learn one of the simplest strategies for understanding poetry: rereading. Reading a poem several times helps readers form a general impression of what the poem is about. Once a reader has a general impression of the subject of the poem, it is easier to understand the poem's meaning.

➤ E. E. Cummings's poem, "if everything happens that can't be done" appears difficult at first. On the first reading, the poem seems a jumble. There's no capitalization, no punctuation, and no discernible rhythm. The poem, however, becomes easier to understand with each rereading.

➤ In terms of poetic style, Cummings's pattern is simple. This is a poem within a poem, or two poems that are joined in meaning. The central poem is formed by the lines that are not enclosed in parentheses. The "outside" poem is a love poem with an upbeat rhythm and a clear and simple rhyme scheme. The second poem—the poem formed by the lines within the parentheses—lacks the clear-cut rhythm of the central poem and has no rhyme scheme. The parenthetical poem is also a love poem, but it is looser, freer, more exuberant. It is, however, linked to the outside poem by rhyme, for example "guess" and "yes."

FOR DISCUSSION AND REFLECTION

Discuss with students their general impressions of Cummings's poem.

➤ What does Cummings's tone or mood seem to be in the poem? (Possible answers: celebratory, playful, exuberant)

➤ What makes this poem difficult to understand the first time you read it? (Possible answers include lack of punctuation and capitalization, parenthetical structure, unusual use of language.)

Writing

QUICK ASSESS

Do students' impressions:

✓ reflect a careful reading of Cummings's poem?

✓ show an attempt to understand the subject of the poem?

Students are asked to write down four things they know for certain about the poem and then one question about the poem they'd like answered.

READING AND WRITING EXTENSIONS

➤ Have students work in pairs to create a poem in two voices. Each student should write a series of lines on the same topic. They should then alternate their lines to create a finished poem in "two voices."

➤ Ask for four or five volunteers to perform dramatic readings of "if everything happens that can't be done." How do these readings change students' views of the poem?

Two Making Sense

Critical Reading

FOCUS

Sharing perceptions, ideas, and questions about a poem can help to clarify the poem's meaning.

BACKGROUND

Reading and rereading a poem is one strategy to aid in understanding the poem's meaning. Another strategy is to share a poem with someone else. A second (or a third or a fourth) reader will be able to offer a slightly different understanding of the poem as a whole, or a slightly different interpretation of a particular line or stanza.

➤ When working with others to decide on a poem's meaning, one strategy is to do a line-by-line or stanza-by-stanza analysis of the poem. One person can read the line or stanza aloud and then stop and ask what it means. Later on, individual comments about parts of the poem can be put together and used to aid in interpreting the poem as a whole.

➤ A line-by-line analysis of "if everything happens that can't be done" is a particularly effective approach because the poem jumps around ["(with a run/skip/around we go yes)"]; because Cummings uses some everyday words in a unique way ("everyanything"); and because he uses a few invented words ("shuter") that each person may define differently.

FOR DISCUSSION AND REFLECTION

Choose one stanza of the poem to analyze with students.

➤ What is Cummings trying to say in this stanza? (Responses will vary. Students should support their responses with quotations from the poem.)

➤ In what ways does this stanza contribute to the overall effect of the poem? (Responses will vary.)

Writing

QUICK ASSESS

Do students:

✔ explain what they think the subject of the poem is?

✔ support their interpretations?

Students are asked to write what they think the poem is about. As a prewriting activity, students will read and comment on other students' observations about the poem.

READING AND WRITING EXTENSIONS

➤ Ask students to work with a partner on some oral readings of "if everything happens that can't be done." One person should read the parenthetical lines and the other should read the "outside" lines. How does a two-person reading affect students' understanding of the poem?

➤ Ask students to return to the comments they made after reading this poem for the first time. Their lists of what they know about the poem can be made longer now. Have them add to their lists, writing everything they know for sure about this poem. Also have them make a note of any questions they still have about the poem.

Three Juxtaposing Texts

Critical Reading

FOCUS

Making connections between two poems can help readers understand and interpret each of the poems.

BACKGROUND

Another strategy for helping readers understand poetry is to see how one poem relates to (and differs from) another. In "Juxtaposing Texts," students are asked to read and compare two poems. What students should notice is that although the two poems are quite different in terms of language and tone, they are remarkably similar in terms of main subject and theme.

➤ Notice first the chief differences between the two poems. Whitman's tone moves from stiff and formal to free and relaxed, while Altaha's tone is much more conversational. Another difference lies in the language the two poets use. Whitman's language has a sophisticated feel to it, while the Apache girl's language is simpler, more childlike ("Have you ever hurt about baskets? / I have. . . . ").

➤ Now notice that although each poem has a different tone and uses different language, the two poems both say essentially the same thing. Whitman's point (that he'd rather look at the stars all by himself, in "the mystical moist night-air . . .") is the same point that Altaha makes in her poem—that she'd rather view life on her own terms, using her own language. Neither Whitman nor Altaha have a high regard for the language of "book learning."

FOR DISCUSSION AND REFLECTION

Discuss with students their responses to the two poems in this lesson.

➤ Which poem do students find more appealing? Why? (Students should support their choices with examples from the poems and connections to their own experiences.)

➤ Which poem seems most similar to "if everything happens that can't be done"? (Responses will vary. Students may suggest that "Have You Ever Hurt About Baskets?" is more similar to the Cummings poem because both poems have an informal, conversational tone.)

Writing

QUICK ASSESS

Do students' responses:

✓ explain the subject of each poem?

✓ explain each author's attitude toward his or her subject?

✓ compare and contrast the three poems?

Students will first write about the connections they see between the two poems. Then they will compare and contrast the poems to a third poem.

READING AND WRITING EXTENSIONS

➤ Ask students to complete a chart that explores the similarities and differences between the three poems. In their charts they might choose to compare elements such as theme, author's intent, language, subject matter, and so on.

➤ Have students write a review of one of the three poems for their school's literary magazine. In their reviews students should explain what they did or did not like about the poem.

Four Using Venn Diagrams

Critical Reading

FOCUS

Examining two or more poems side-by-side can help the reader compare and contrast elements such as style, tone, and subject matter.

BACKGROUND

In Lesson Four, "Using Venn Diagrams," students are asked to consider again what "When I Heard the Learn'd Astronomer," "Have You Ever Hurt About Baskets?" and "if everything happens that can't be done" have in common. The Venn diagrams they make will help them keep track of the similarities and differences between the poems.

➤ All three of these poems are written in *free verse* (poetry that makes use of unpatterned, irregular rhythms rather than uniform metric feet). In free verse, poets often use repetition or sound devices to bind lines together and create mood. Notice, for example, Whitman's repetition of the "When I" structure, Altaha's repetition of "Have you ever . . ." and Cummings's repetition of words such as "everything," "anything," and "one."

➤ In this lesson students are also asked to note how the poems are different. They are different in terms of language (Whitman uses a more formal English, while Cummings and Altaha rely on more colloquial English). The poems are also different in terms of mood: the Cummings poem has an exuberant, celebratory tone; the Apache girl's tone is slow and mournful; and the tone of the Whitman poem beginhs as thoughtful and ponderous, but ends in relief. And although all three poems are written in free verse, they do have stylistic differences: the Cummings poem feels much more modern than the other two, while Altaha's poem appears to be the most straightforward.

FOR DISCUSSION AND REFLECTION

Ask students to compare and contrast their attitudes toward the three poems.

➤ Which poem did they find easiest to read? Which poem did they find most difficult? Why? (Accept responses that students can support with examples from the poems and their own experience.)

➤ Which poem or poet might they want to return to in the future? Why? (Responses will vary.)

Writing

QUICK ASSESS

Do students' comparisons:

✓ take all three poems into account ?

✓ examine the poems in terms of structure, speaker, and language?

✓ examine each poet's perspective?

Students will write about how the three poems differ in subject, structure, language, and perspective. As a prewriting activity, students will compare and contrast the poems using a Venn Diagram.

READING AND WRITING EXTENSIONS

➤ Ask students to write a poem of their own in which they imitate either Cummings, Whitman, or Altaha.

➤ Have students write a speech in which they introduce either Cummings, Whitman, or Altaha to an audience not familiar with the poet's work. Speeches should focus on the poet's style.

Five Selecting Strategies

Critical Reading

FOCUS

There are many ways to approach a work of poetry. Poetry is easier to understand and enjoy when the reader is aware of and utilizes various interpretive strategies.

BACKGROUND

In this lesson, students are asked to read two different poems and then decide which strategy they will use to help them interpret the poems' meanings. Before they begin, you may want to review with them some of the strategies they've explored: rereading; asking questions and drawing conclusions; juxtaposing texts; and comparing and contrasting poems.

➤ For the grasshopper poem, any of these strategies will work. This is an example of a poem that is confusing on the first reading, but becomes clearer when it's reread a few times. Once readers understand that Cummings is in fact talking about a grasshopper, they'll see that he uses an odd structure (and free verse) in order to imitate the "leA!p" of the insect he describes.

➤ In "The Negro Speaks of Rivers," Langston Hughes celebrates the longevity and courage of Africans and African Americans by comparing them to the "Ancient, dusky rivers" of the Euphrates (regarded by some as the "cradle" of civilization), and the Nile, Congo, and Mississippi Rivers. For this poem, any of the strategies students have learned so far will help them interpret its meaning.

FOR DISCUSSION AND REFLECTION

Ask students to summarize the techniques they used to understand the two poems.

➤ What aspects of the Hughes poem and the Cummings poem do students find easy to understand? (Students' responses should include specific examples from the poems.)

➤ How did having strategies to help them in their interpretations affect how they felt about interpreting the poems? (Accept reasonable responses.)

Writing

QUICK ASSESS

Do students' writings:

✓ show they understand the poem's meaning?

✓ offer support for their interpretations?

✓ describe different strategies for interpreting poetry?

Students are asked to write a summary of one of the poems they read in this unit. They are then asked to analyze the strategies they used to get at the meaning of the poems.

READING AND WRITING EXTENSIONS

➤ Ask students to write a free-verse poem that explores a subject they find interesting or important. Offer them the option of using a poem they've read in this unit as a model for their style.

➤ Have students write a "Poet's Corner" column for their school newspaper in which they recommend one of the poems in this unit to the student body. The columnist will need to explain why the poem's subject or theme is relevant to students' lives.

THE USE OF QUESTIONS

Unit Overview

By reading and responding to a variety of texts, students will examine the value of questions (how to ask them, where they lead, what they provoke) and how authors use questions to deepen the meaning of their writing.

LITERATURE FOCUS

Lesson	Literature
1. Questions and Answers	**Donald Justice**, "Twenty Questions" (Poetry)
2. Simple Questions, Complex Answers	**Pablo Neruda**, Poems VII, XVI, XXIV from *The Book of Questions* (Poetry)
3. Questions and Antecedents	**Pablo Neruda**, Poems XXII, XLIV from *The Book of Questions* (Poetry)
4. Questions and Similes	**Mary Oliver**, "Some Questions You Might Ask" (Poetry)
5. Questions and Paradoxes	**Mary Oliver**, "What Is It?" (Poetry)

READING FOCUS

1. Writers sometimes use questions as a way of making remarks or statements. Writing your own question poem helps you understand this technique.
2. Writers often use questions to explore their own ideas. Even simple or childlike questions can be extremely deep or even unanswerable.
3. Good readers analyze a poem word-by-word and sentence-by-sentence in order to understand the meaning of the whole.
4. Writers often use metaphors and similes to reflect on questions about large, abstract ideas. The images in the comparisons allow a reader to see and feel the ideas more clearly.
5. Writers use questions to present and explore paradoxes. In this way, they can expand their search or their understanding of the apparent contradiction.

WRITING FOCUS

1. Write a poem using the format of the game "Twenty Questions."
2. Write a poem that explores a meaningful issue by posing a series of questions.
3. Analyze one stanza of a poem closely and write about its meaning.
4. Extend the author's poem by writing additional lines that include similes.
5. Compare how sketching a poem and reading it in prose form affect understanding.

One Questions and Answers

Critical Reading

FOCUS

Sometimes it is more effective to pose a question about an idea than to make a direct statement about it. When a writer poses a question, the reader becomes an active participant in exploring the idea and finding the answer.

BACKGROUND

The ancient Greek philosopher Socrates first proposed the idea that the most important part of teaching and learning is asking questions. In "Questions and Answers," students are invited to read—and solve—a riddle poem by Donald Justice.

➤ The poem is similar to the game of "Twenty Questions" in that the speaker of the poem does indeed ask twenty questions. And, viewed as a whole, the questions in the poem all have the same purpose as the questions in the game: they are all attempts to figure out the person, place, or thing described.

➤ Although Justice does ask twenty questions, and the questions are designed to help figure out the solution to the riddle, this poem is actually quite different from the standard game of "Twenty Questions." Notice, for example, how odd Justice's questions are: "Do you recall the word for carnation?" would not be typical for the game "Twenty Questions." And as the "guesser" in the poem asks more and more questions, he seems to be moving away from rather than moving toward a solution to the riddle.

FOR DISCUSSION AND REFLECTION

Discuss with students why asking questions is such an important part of learning.

➤ How does asking questions help us see things we hadn't thought of before? (Possible response: Asking questions opens our minds to new interpretations and ways of looking at things.)

➤ What makes for an effective question? How can we tell if a question is not effective? (Possible answers: Effective questions are clear, precise, and direct; a question that is not effective often results in an unclear answer.)

Writing

QUICK ASSESS

Are students' poems:

✔ written in a "Twenty Questions" format?

✔ creative?

✔ well-written?

Students are asked to make up their own twenty-questions poems. As a prewriting activity, they'll examine the techniques Justice uses in his poem.

READING AND WRITING EXTENSIONS

➤ Discuss the Socratic method and empirical reasoning with students. Have them compare Socrates' method of using questions to refine and hone ideas, with how Justice is using questions in his poem.

➤ Ask students to write a news or feature story for their school newspaper. As a part of the assignment, students will need to conduct at least one interview. Students should prepare their interview questions beforehand.

Two Simple Questions, Complex Answers

Critical Reading

FOCUS
Writers sometimes pose questions that look simple on the surface, but that turn out to be more complex when the reader examines them closely or attempts to answer them.

BACKGROUND
In true Socratic fashion, writers will often pose a series of questions in order to help the reader think about complex or controversial issues. Sometimes the author has an opinion about an issue and uses questions as a way of helping the reader see his or her point of view.

➤ Notice the questions Nobel Prize-winner Pablo Neruda asks in these three poems. In each poem, he asks a series of seemingly simple questions that are in fact quite difficult to answer. Neruda's questions are difficult because they explore abstract concepts such as human relationships, war, peace, and love.

➤ In "XXIV," for example, Neruda asks the simple question, "Is 4 the same 4 for everybody?" Although this is the first line of the poem, we don't need to read many more lines to figure out that Neruda is not writing verse about mathematics. Instead, he uses mathematical questions as a means of exploring the differences between humans.

➤ Consider also the tone of these three poems. Because the questions appear so simple, the verse has a childlike quality that Neruda may have intended as an ironic comment on the complexity of the issues he presents.

FOR DISCUSSION AND REFLECTION
Invite students to discuss Neruda's three poems.

➤ How does the mood of "XXIV" differ from the other two poems? (The mood is darker and more serious.)

➤ How is "VII" similar to "XVI"? (Possible answer: They both draw on elements of nature.)

➤ Which of Neruda's questions made you stop and think? Why? (Responses will vary.)

Writing

QUICK ASSESS
Do students' poems:

✓ explore issues of importance?

✓ include questions from each category on the chart?

✓ show careful thought and creativity?

Students are asked to write a question poem in which they explore an issue that is important to them. They will use Neruda's poems as models.

READING AND WRITING EXTENSIONS
➤ Ask students to evaluate their own question poems. What do they like best about their poems? What do they like least? Are they satisfied with the ways they expressed their thoughts?

➤ Ask students to create a collage that reflects these three Neruda poems. For their collages, students can use words and pictures from magazines as well as their own words and art. The collages should reflect the subject, tone, style, and themes of the poetry.

Three Questions and Antecedents

Critical Reading

FOCUS

To be understood as a whole, many poems must be analyzed in parts—word-by-word, line-by-line, and stanza-by-stanza.

BACKGROUND

In Lesson Three, "Questions and Antecedents," students focus on the relationship between the questions the author asks and the underlying meaning of the author's work. As they examine two more poems by Pablo Neruda, students will find that a line-by-line or even a word-by-word analysis is a useful approach. The poems "XXII" and "XLIV" seem challenging on the first reading simply because Neruda uses no antecedents for his pronouns. After the reader assigns a noun for each pronoun, however, individual lines are much easier to follow.

➤ Notice how the questions Neruda asks have a mournful quality to them. The poem "XLIV" in particular sounds like one long lament, mostly because of the alternating "why" and "does" questions. The childlike simplicity of the questions' construction matches exactly the lament over a lost childhood.

➤ "XXII" is also in many ways a poem of mourning, though in this case, the speaker mourns the end of a love so powerful it was able to change the texture of the landscape, the smell of the sky, and the color of the water.

FOR DISCUSSION AND REFLECTION

Discuss with students why many people find poetry more challenging than fiction.

➤ How does a poet's language generally differ from a novelist's? (Poetic language often relies on symbolism, imagery, etc., to convey an idea rather than on direct statements.)

➤ What are some techniques a reader can use to make a poem easier to understand? (Possible answers: breaking the poem into smaller parts, rereading the poem)

Writing

QUICK ASSESS

Do students' analyses:

✔ offer interpretations of Neruda's style?

✔ offer interpretations of the stanza's meanings?

✔ demonstrate an understanding of both poems?

Students are asked to determine antecedents for the pronouns Neruda uses and then decide on the meaning of the two poems.

READING AND WRITING EXTENSIONS

➤ Now that they have read at least five poems by Pablo Neruda, students should have some sense of the characteristics of his poetic style. Ask them to write a list of the characteristics they associate with Neruda's poetry. Their lists should focus on stylistic and thematic elements in his verse.

➤ Ask students to read some additional poetry by Pablo Neruda. Have them choose one poem to analyze line-by-line. They can then read the poem and present their thoughts on it to the class.

Four Questions and Similes

Critical Reading

FOCUS

Poets often deal with abstract concepts, such as love and death. One way of making these concepts more accessible and concrete is to explore them through the use of direct comparisons or *similes*.

BACKGROUND

In this lesson, students will explore how a writer can use similes to present abstractions such as peace, love, or hatred. In her poem "Some Questions You Might Ask," Mary Oliver creates something that is tangible from the intangible concept of the soul. She accomplishes this through her use of similes.

➤ A simile is a comparison between two basically unlike things that nonetheless have something in common. Most similes use compare/contrast words such as *like* or *as*. In this poem, Oliver poses a series of questions that establish that the soul is a mystery; with her similes, she shows us that if we think of the soul in terms of something we do understand, such as "the wings of a moth in the beak of the owl," it is easier to understand what the soul *might* be like.

➤ Interestingly, Oliver's similes allow her to answer her own questions. By comparing the soul to elements in nature, she reveals her idea that the soul is a thing of beauty—fragile like the wings of a moth, yet as strong as iron and as imposing as a maple tree.

FOR DISCUSSION AND REFLECTION

Ask students to discuss Oliver's use of imagery and sensory language.

➤ What do most of the images in the poem compare the soul to? (Comparisons are made between the soul and various aspects of nature.)

➤ What are some examples of sensory language in the poem? (Possible answers include "white wings," "darkness," "iceberg," "blue iris," "shining leaves," "roses," and "lemons.")

➤ Does Oliver's use of similes make the concept of the soul easier to grasp and explore? Why? (Possible answer: The similes make the concept easier to grasp by allowing the reader to visualize the soul in various concrete ways.)

Writing

QUICK ASSESS
Do students' extensions:

✓ demonstrate an understanding of similes?

✓ imitate Oliver's style?

✓ show careful reflection and creativity?

Students are asked to extend Oliver's poem by writing additional lines that include similes. As a prewriting activity, they'll analyze Oliver's use of similes in her poem.

READING AND WRITING EXTENSIONS

➤ Ask students to compare Oliver's poem to one of Pablo Neruda's from Lessons Two or Three. How are the two poems similar and different in terms of language, style, tone, and the kinds of questions asked?

➤ As a class, brainstorm some similes for abstract concepts such as *love, hatred, peace,* and *friendship*. Students can then choose one simile to explain in a paragraph.

Five Questions and Paradoxes

Critical Reading

FOCUS

Sometimes writers explore a paradox—an apparent contradiction—by asking the reader questions. This prompts the readers to look at the topic or idea in a new way and to see possibilities they may not have considered before.

BACKGROUND

In this lesson students will explore how questions and paradoxes are used in writing. A paradox is a statement that may be true but seems to say two opposite things. One of the reasons authors use paradoxes in their writing is to guarantee (rather than assume or hope) that the reader will stop and take a moment to figure out what the author is saying. Mary Oliver creates a poem-length paradox in " What Is It?" in order to invite the reader to think about the paradoxical relationship between life and death.

➤ In her poem Oliver presents the paradox that an important part of living is dying. Why is it, Oliver asks, that we often feel the safest from harm when we are most at risk? The salamanders in the pond, "breast-stroking / like little green dwarves / under the roof of the rich, / iron-colored water," are actually at great risk from a being who has "fire-colored eyes." In these lines lies another paradox: why is it that the younger we are, the less likely we are to listen to those who know what's best for us?

FOR DISCUSSION AND REFLECTION

Discuss with students the paradoxes Oliver sets up in her poem.

➤ What central paradox does Oliver explore in her poem? (She explores the paradox that life ends in death and that death begins with life.)

➤ How does Oliver's use of paradoxes affect the tone of her poem? (Oliver's paradoxes are a roundabout, meandering way of getting at questions. As a result, the poem has a meandering, slow, or dreamy quality.)

Writing

QUICK ASSESS

Do students' explanations:

✓ discuss the three parts of the poem?

✓ explore how visualizing the poem affects understanding?

✓ show understanding of the paradox Oliver presents?

Students are asked to explain how visualizing the three parts of the poem helps them resolve the paradox. As a prewriting activity, they'll draw three different pictures to represent the beginning of the poem, the poem's action, and the end of the poem.

READING AND WRITING EXTENSIONS

➤ What are some paradoxes that students find bothersome or interesting? For example, students might ask: why is it that the foods that taste the best are the worst for our health? Ask students to work in small groups to come up with a list of paradoxes.

➤ Have students look back over the poems they read in this unit. Then ask them to describe in a paragraph or two which poet's style they found most appealing and why.

WRITING FROM MODELS

Unit Overview

An important part of learning to write well is learning to read well. As readers, we consciously or unconsciously look for writing styles that appeal to us—that we might want to imitate when we write. In "Writing from Models," students will learn the value of looking carefully at the writing styles of authors.

LITERATURE FOCUS

Lesson	Literature
1. Spinoff Modeling	**Kathleen Raine**, "The Unloved" (Poetry)
2. Description Through Detail	**George Ella Lyon**, "Where I'm From" (Poetry)
3. Repetition	**Gary Gildner**, "My Father After Work" (Poetry)
4. Extended Metaphor	**George Macbeth**, "Marshall" (Poetry)
5. Word-for-Word Modeling	**Robert Frost**, "Acquainted with the Night" (Poetry)

READING FOCUS

1. Writing a spinoff poem allows you the freedom of writing your own poem and the discipline of following someone else's model.
2. Creating categories for the images in a writer's work helps you focus on the important details.
3. Writers repeat words or phrases on purpose. It helps them make a point and reinforce it.
4. An extended metaphor is a comparison carried on throughout a large portion of a piece of writing.
5. Emulating helps you examine an author's intent, point of view, and sentence structure. At the same time, you are creating your own distinct style.

WRITING FOCUS

1. Write a poem modeled on Kathleen Raine's "The Unloved."
2. Write a "Where I'm From" poem, modeled on George Ella Lyon's poem.
3. Write a description of someone in a poem, using repetition.
4. Write a poem describing something with an extended metaphor.
5. Write an emulation of a Robert Frost poem.

One Spinoff Modeling

Critical Reading

FOCUS

Kathleen Raine:

"I am the white bird
Flying away from land
I am the horizon."

BACKGROUND

In Lesson One students are asked to borrow the words and structure of Kathleen Raine's poem "The Unloved" for poems of their own. The model's short lines and concrete images make it an excellent template for novice writers.

➤ Students will want to pay particular attention to the way Raine piles image upon image without need of transitional phrases or explanation in her poem. Each stanza is a kind of photographic snapshot from a movie about the experience of not being loved. The pictures Raine creates are thematically related yet visually distinct. In literature we call these images "metaphors" (a figure of speech in which a name or descriptive term is transferred to some object different from, but analogous to, that to which it is properly applied).

FOR DISCUSSION AND REFLECTION

Discuss with students the style and structure of Kathleen Raine's poem.

➤ How does the fact that the poem is written in the present tense affect the reader? (It makes the experience of the poem more immediate.)

➤How would the substitution of similes (the comparison of one thing with another using "like" or "as") for the metaphors affect the tone of the poem? "I am like the empty air. / I am like a drifting cloud." (It puts the narrator at a greater distance from the image.)

➤Ask students to choose the stanza that spoke most directly to them about the feeling of being unloved. Have them explain why to a partner. Go through the poem stanza by stanza to see which ones were chosen most often. Discuss why this might be.

Writing

QUICK ASSESS

Do students' poems:

✓ use Raine's structure?

✓ contain examples of figurative and sensory language?

✓ have a focus?

Students are asked to write a spinoff poem from Kathleen Raine's "The Unloved." Assist them in getting started by creating a class poem on the board with the word "Afraid." Once students have a sense of how a poem can be created from a list of metaphors, they will find it easier to write their own.

READING AND WRITING EXTENSIONS

➤ Ask students to read a poem by one of their classmates and make a series of sketches beside each stanza the way they did for Raine's poem.

➤ Write a letter to Kathleen Raine thanking her for the use of her poem. Have them enclose their own poems.

Two Description Through Detail

Critical Reading

FOCUS
George Ella Lyon on her hopes for her writing:

"Early on I wanted to be a neon sign maker and I still hope to make words glow."

BACKGROUND

"Description Through Detail" examines the ways in which a poet uses detail to help the reader visualize the people, places, and things described. George Ella Lyon's poem "Where I'm From" is full of the kinds of details that really capture a reader's attention and make a piece of writing memorable.

➤ Notice the many kinds of details Lyon offers. She describes aspects of nature (the forsythia bush and Dutch elm), her family (her grandfather and father), and her religious upbringing ("I'm from He restoreth my soul / with a cottonball lamb / and ten verses I can say myself"). She also explores other people's attitudes toward her, the things she likes to eat, the smell of the clothes she wore. Notice how Lyons never tells us exactly where she's from. She trusts in the reader's ability to infer the location from the details provided.

➤ Although Lyon offers the same kinds of specific details about everything she describes, she describes some places and people and things in more depth. Notice how she merely mentions the "the forsythia bush," but speaks of the Dutch elm's "long gone limbs I remember / as if they were my own." She continues this pattern—a few details. . . more details. . . and still more details—throughout the poem.

FOR DISCUSSION AND REFLECTION

Discuss with students what they can infer about the speaker of the poem.

➤ Where is she from? What does she like? What does she dislike? What is most important to her? (Responses will vary.)

Writing

QUICK ASSESS
Do students:

✓ use details from several different categories?

✓ use figurative language?

✓ use imagery?

Students are asked to write their own "Where I'm From" poems. As a prewriting activity, they'll categorize the details Lyon uses in her poem. They'll also decide on five categories of their own and then write details that fit those categories.

READING AND WRITING EXTENSIONS

➤ Ask students to write a one-paragraph biographical sketch of George Ella Lyon using what they know and what they have inferred from "Where I'm From."

➤ In many ways, Lyon's poem is similar to Donald Justice's poem "Twenty Questions" on page 180. Review with students the characteristics of a riddle poem. Then ask them to write a riddle poem about where they are from.

Three Repetition

Critical Reading

FOCUS

Writers use repetition to add emphasis and richness to their prose or verse. It is the essential unifying element of poetry.

BACKGROUND

Lesson Three is designed to help students understand the effect repetition can have on a piece of writing. Think, for example, of the repetition Edgar Allen Poe used in "The Raven" ("Nevermore . . .") or the repetition Martin Luther King, Jr. used in his "I Have a Dream" speech. In both cases, the use of repetition made the writing more vivid and memorable. It also served to draw attention to the ideas these writers wanted to express.

➤ To help students see the effects repetition can have on writing, they will read a poem by Gary Gildner. In "My Father After Work," Gildner uses repetition as a means of creating the quiet, pensive mood of reflection and recollection that is such an important part of his poem. Notice how Gildner begins each stanza with "Putting out the candles. . . ." The repetition of this phrase has a hypnotic effect on the reader. We are charmed by its simplicity and interested in its implications.

➤ Gildner uses repetition ("I think of winter"; "I think of going away") to help maintain the rhythmic flow of the poem. This inter-stanza repetition is a way of encouraging the reader to follow along behind the speaker just as he follows along behind his father.

FOR DISCUSSION AND REFLECTION

Discuss with students the various elements of a poet's craft.

➤ What are some characteristics of a poem? (Possible responses: rhyme, lines, meter and rhythm, figures of speech, etc.)

➤ In what ways does poetry differ from prose? (Poetry is more focused than prose. Its language is concentrated and precise.)

Writing

QUICK ASSESS
Do students:

✓ imitate aspects of Gildner's style?

✓ use repetition to set the mood and tie the poem together?

✓ use symbolism, figurative language, and vivid details?

Students are asked to write a poem using repetition. As a prewriting activity, they'll examine Gildner's use of repetition and then answer a series of questions about possible subjects for their own poems.

READING AND WRITING EXTENSIONS

➤ Invite students to think about how the tone, mood, and style of Gildner's poem would change if the line "Putting out the candles" were written as something else. For example, how would the poem be different if the first line of every stanza were "Putting out the cat. . ."?

➤ Ask students: what other kinds of writers (besides poets) use repetition in their writing? Have students thumb through their literature anthologies and read material from home to find examples of repetition. When they've finished their research, lead a class discussion about the various kinds of repetition they've found.

Four **Extended Metaphor**

Critical Reading

FOCUS

A metaphor is a comparison between two things that are basically different but nonetheless share some similar qualities. In an extended metaphor, a writer presents the metaphor and then carefully strengthens it throughout the entire work.

BACKGROUND

Lesson Four, "Extended Metaphor," is designed to show students the various ways of creating a metaphor—and the various ways of extending the metaphor they have created. Before they try writing a metaphor of their own, students are asked to read George Macbeth's poem "Marshall."

➤ In "Marshall" Macbeth introduces his metaphor of the bean in the first stanza and then builds on it, or extends it, throughout the poem. The effect is a poem that is witty and different—far more unique than a poem that simply describes the kind of person Marshall is. In this case (as is the case with most figurative language), Macbeth's extended metaphor serves to add freshness and vitality to his writing.

FOR DISCUSSION AND REFLECTION

Discuss with students how Macbeth's metaphor adds humor and seriousness to the poem.

➤ What's strange about comparing a person to a bean? (Responses will vary, but should focus on the incongruity. Macbeth's meaning is a bit unexpected because we generally refer to people as "string beans" or "bean poles" because of height.)

➤ What are some reasons Macbeth might have wanted to make a comparison? What does this tell you about his personality? (Responses will vary.)

Writing

QUICK ASSESS

Do students:

✓ create an extended metaphor?

✓ use Macbeth's poem as a model for their style?

✓ demonstrate careful thought and creativity?

Students are asked to write poems in which they use an extended metaphor. As a prewriting activity, they will think about some vegetable comparisons they might make. You might encourage students to work together in small groups when they begin developing their metaphors. Group members can read each other's work and offer comments and suggestions.

READING AND WRITING EXTENSIONS

➤ Have students write an outline of a short story starring Marshall as the main character. Their outlines should identify elements of the setting, the conflict, and the resolution of conflict.

➤ Ask students to write a character sketch of Marshall. What is his personality like? What interests him? What bores him?

Five Word-for-Word Modeling

Critical Reading

FOCUS
Emulating is a useful technique for understanding the message a poet is trying to get across.

BACKGROUND
Robert Frost had an amazing gift for language and an equally amazing ability to construct rhyme and create rhythm. Students will begin the lesson by reading Frost's poem "Acquainted with the Night." As they read, encourage them to listen for the sound of Frost's words, and the rhythmic pattern of his lines.

➤ In "Acquainted with the Night" Frost employs an *ababcbcdc dadaa* end rhyme and a standard iambic pentameter metrical pattern. (In iambic pentameter each line has five metrical feet. Most feet in the line contain an unaccented syllable followed by an accented syllable):

> I have / been one / ac quaint / ted with / the night.

> I have / walked out / in rain / and back / in rain.

➤ In "Acquainted with the Night," Frost's use of the familiar iambic pentameter pattern makes the poem seem comfortable and familiar. This is not a difficult poem to read, nor, the reader assumes, a difficult one to understand. Frost uses repetition for that same purpose.

FOR DISCUSSION AND REFLECTION
Discuss with students what the speaker means when he says he is "acquainted with the night."

➤ What is the literal meaning of the phrase? (It literally means he has seen the dark hours of each day.)

➤ What is the figurative meaning of the phrase? (Figuratively, the poet is discussing the darker aspects of the human condition and soul.)

➤ Does the phrase conjure a positive or negative image? How so? (It conjures a negative image of the things in life we try to hide from.)

Writing

QUICK ASSESS

Are students' emulations:

✓ similar in form to Frost's poem?

✓ carefully done?

✓ creative and interesting?

Students are asked to write an emulation of the poem "Acquainted with the Night." Before they begin, they will do a line-by-line analysis of Frost's poem in order to examine his techniques for creating rhyme, rhythm, and meter. They'll also spend time thinking about his language—his word choices, his attention to detail, and his use of imagery, simile, and metaphor.

READING AND WRITING EXTENSIONS
➤ Ask students to write a paragraph or two in which they assess their abilities to emulate Frost's style. What did they find easy? What did they find difficult? How would they rate their work? Explain.

➤ Invite students to write a parody of Frost's poem. Some titles they might consider include:

"Acquainted with the Light," "Acquainted with Your Plight," "Acquainted with a Kite," or "Accustomed to your Sight"

Unit Overview

In this unit, students are invited to take an in-depth look at one of today's most popular Chicano writers, Rudolfo Anaya. A poet, novelist, playwright, and essayist, Anaya has won numerous awards for his work. Students will be asked to read and respond to excerpts from two essays and from Anaya's most-popular work, the novel *Bless Me, Ultima*. They will explore aspects of his voice and writing style, as well as the emphasis he places on his cultural heritage.

LITERATURE FOCUS

Lesson	Literature
1. Finding a Voice	from "An American Chicano in King Arthur's Court" (Nonfiction)
2. The Importance of the Past	from "A Celebration of Grandfathers" (Nonfiction)
3. The Importance of Values	from "A Celebration of Grandfathers" (Nonfiction)
4. The Art of Storytelling	from *Bless Me, Ultima* (Novel)
5. Finding a Style	

READING FOCUS

1. A writer's voice develops from a series of influences. You must know who you are to write well.
2. Writing about the past can give meaning to the present.
3. An author's ideas about values are often implied rather than stated explicitly.
4. Stories often connect listeners with traditions and a sense of the connections among human beings.
5. Writers' experiences and values influence all facets of their writing style.

WRITING FOCUS

1. Create a pie chart that reflects the influences on Anaya's style and voice.
2. Write a short essay describing what you have learned from your grandparents or other people of that generation.
3. Write a short piece analyzing the author's meaning and how he supports his ideas.
4. Write a paragraph describing what you think are the strengths and weaknesses of writing like an oral storyteller.
5. Write a letter describing Anaya's writing style and sense of tradition.

One Finding a Voice

Critical Reading

FOCUS

Rudolfo Anaya on the richness of his culture:

"[If] we forget that sense of the sacred and are drawn more into the world of the material, we lose touch with a very important aspect of ourselves, who we are as spiritually aware persons, and that we have a past history that is full of beautiful myths and stories that talk about that spirituality...."

BACKGROUND

Every writer's voice, or writing style, is unique. No two writers have exactly the same style, though two or more writers may share some of the same stylistic techniques. In Lesson One, "Finding a Voice," students will read about Rudolfo Anaya's quest to find a writing style he felt comfortable with. Anaya explains in his essay "An American Chicano in King Arthur's Court" that although he knew he had stories to tell, he found himself without a voice to tell them. He felt certain that the traditional rhetoric he learned in school (the style of "King Arthur's Court") was not suitable for a Chicano who wanted to write in his voice using his characters and his indigenous symbols.

➤ Notice how clearly we can hear Anaya's voice. In all of his writing there are elements of the mystical, the unexplained, the legends of his family and his people. In this essay he speaks of "Ultima . . . that strong, old curandera of my first novel . . . came to me one night and pointed the way." This juxtaposition of realism with mysticism is one of the most important parts of Anaya's voice.

➤ We can also hear Anaya's voice in his use of figurative language. He uses imagery throughout the essay, and relies heavily on metaphors to make his writing vivid. When he speaks of diving "deep into the lake of your subconsciousness," he uses the kind of simple and straightforward metaphor for which he is known.

FOR DISCUSSION AND REFLECTION

Discuss with students how an author may have difficulty finding his or her "voice."

➤ Why is it important for a writer to find a voice? (When we say an author has found a voice, what we mean is that he or she is able to produce natural, honest sentences, which express what the writer wants. The writer's voice is an important element of a personal writing style.)

➤ What are the characteristics of an author's voice? (There are many characteristics of an author's voice: word choice, rhythm, diction, tone, mood, and so on.)

Writing

QUICK ASSESS

Do students:

✓ understand the concept of an author's "voice"?

✓ note the characteristics of Anaya's voice?

✓ account for the forces that shaped Anaya's voice?

Students create a pie chart that reflects the many forces that contributed to Anaya's voice.

READING AND WRITING EXTENSIONS

➤ Ask students to make a pie chart that reflects the forces that shaped their writing styles. When they've finished, have them write a short essay in which they compare their pie charts to the charts they made about Anaya.

➤ Working as a class, brainstorm with students a list of writers with distinctive voices. (Students might suggest, for example, that Ernest Hemingway and Edgar Allan Poe have distinctive voices.) When you've finished the list, ask students to choose an author to research and then report on. Their reports should focus on the author's voice and the ways in which it is distinctive.

Two The Importance of the Past

Critical Reading

BACKGROUND
In "A Celebration of Grandfathers," Anaya describes how important his grandfather was to him as a child. Anaya's *abuelo* showed Anaya how to love the simple things in life: the whispering wind, a ride in a wagon, the smell of the orchards and fields of his homeland. Anaya's *abuelo* was a man of peace who never lifted a hand or raised his voice in anger. He was, according to his dutiful grandson, a man who was close to perfect.

➤ Anaya's tone in his essay is slow, quiet, and peaceful—almost as peaceful, in fact, as his beloved *abuelo* was. Notice for example, the simple beauty of a sentence such as: "My grandfather touched me, looked up into the sky and whispered, 'Pray for rain.'" Anaya maintains this peaceful tone throughout his writing.

➤ In his essay, Anaya has several points he wants to make about his grandfather (and *los abuelitos* everywhere). According to Anaya, today's "sons and daughters are breaking with the past, putting aside *los abuelitos*." Anaya is bothered by this because he thinks it presents a terrible threat to the integrity of his people's heritage. He sees the young leaving old values behind. Anaya reminds his readers that we still have much to learn from the "old people," and that we must listen carefully to what they have to say.

FOR DISCUSSION AND REFLECTION
Discuss with students the theme of Anaya's essay.

➤ What did Anaya learn from his grandfather? (Responses will vary, but should focus around respect and love for nature, an understanding of life and its pleasures and pains, and respect for the older generation.)

➤ Do you agree or disagree with what Anaya says the "old ones" can teach the young? Explain. (Responses will vary.)

Writing

QUICK ASSESS
Are students' explanations:

✓ thorough?

✓ clear?

✓ well-written and interesting?

Students are asked to explain Anaya's remarks about the "old ones." As a prewriting activity, they will complete a chart about the lessons the grandfather taught Anaya.

READING AND WRITING EXTENSIONS
➤ Ask students to write a descriptive essay about a person who is important to them. Remind them to use details and figurative language in their writing. If they like, they can model their style on Anaya's essay.

➤ Invite students to respond to Anaya's essay in a journal entry. Do they agree with his view? Why or why not? Should they take the time to stop and listen to the *abuelitos* of the world? Why or why not?

Three The Importance of Values

Critical Reading

George Santayana on aging:

"The young man who has not wept is a savage, and the old man who will not laugh is a fool."

BACKGROUND

In this section of his essay, Anaya continues his celebration of *los viejitos*, though he is careful to remind us that we shouldn't romanticize old age because it can be a time of illness and pain, as it was for Anaya's *abuelo*. Above all else, Anaya tells us, we need to remember that *los viejitos* can be "young at heart, but in their own way, with their own dignity."

➤ Earlier in "A Celebration of Grandfathers," Anaya presented his concern that today's sons and daughters are breaking with the past. In this section of his essay, he returns to this concern, but this time approaches it on a more personal level. On a trip to Puerto de Luna, his grandfather's home, Anaya asks himself: "As I plow and plant my words, do I nurture as my grandfather did in his fields and orchards?" With this question, Anaya shows us that he is concerned not only about his reader's values, but about his own values as well.

➤ In the conclusion of the essay, Anaya changes the tenor of his discussion by posing yet another question to his readers: How do we make certain that the cultural values *los viejitos* embraced continue to be honored in future generations? What's most interesting about this question is that although Anaya waits until the end of the essay to ask it, he in fact answered it with the first sentence of the essay: *"Buenos días le de Dios, abuelo."*

FOR DISCUSSION AND REFLECTION

Discuss with students the reasons Anaya believes it's so important to show *respeto* to the elderly.

➤ What is the significance of the phrase *"Buenos días le de Dios"*? (It is a sign of respect and acknowledgment of the older generation.)

➤ Anaya tells his readers to respect their elders. Why might some people find this advice difficult to follow? (There are always clashes between the values and ways of life of different generations.)

Writing

QUICK ASSESS

Do students:

✔ show an understanding of Anaya's questions?

✔ explain Anaya's answers?

✔ offer support for their interpretations?

Students are asked to complete a chart in which they analyze one of the questions Anaya asks in his essay.

READING AND WRITING EXTENSIONS

➤ Invite students to complete a second chart, this time finding an answer to a different question from Anaya's essay. When they finish, they can discuss their work with those students who analyzed the same question.

➤ Have students reread the Anaya excerpt from Lesson Two and compare it to the Anaya excerpt from Lesson Three. Do they see any differences in tone or writing style? What clues do they have that the second excerpt is a continuation of the first?

Four The Art of Storytelling

Critical Reading

FOCUS

Mario Vargas Llosa from "The Storyteller":

"Storytelling can be something more than mere entertainment, something primordial, something that the very existence of a people may depend on."

BACKGROUND

In Lesson Four, "The Art of Storytelling," students are introduced to Anaya's fiction. Anaya represents the "new" generation of his culture's storytellers. Although the oral tradition of their ancestors has given way to the printed word, writers like Anaya continue to use many of the oral storyteller's techniques in their writing. In his writing, Anaya has a keen sense of audience and a skillful way of maintaining interest in the story he wants to tell or the point he wants to make. In this excerpt from his novel *Bless Me, Ultima*, Anaya borrows several techniques from the oral tradition.

➤ Notice how the storyteller, Samuel, is careful to engage his listener before beginning his story. " 'Have you ever fished for the carp of the river?'. . . 'No,' I answered, 'I do not fish for carp. It is bad luck.' 'Do you know why?' he asked and raised an eyebrow." In the oral tradition, storytellers often interrupt themselves in order to gauge and rekindle the reader's interest.

➤ Like all good storytellers, Samuel cues his listener that he has an important story to tell and explains its history. " 'I will tell you a story,' Samuel said after a long silence, 'a story that was told to my father by Jasón's Indian.' "

FOR DISCUSSION AND REFLECTION

Discuss with students the techniques used by storytellers.

➤ What is the storyteller's (Samuel's) attitude towards the story? (reverential) What is his attitude towards Antonio? (kindly and instructive)

➤ In the middle of the story Antonio asks a question that Samuel cannot answer. Why is this an effective storytelling technique? (Good stories often have places that invite listeners to speculate.)

Writing

QUICK ASSESS
Do students:

✔ correctly identify the elements Anaya borrows from the oral tradition?

✔ offer possible reasons why Anaya might have wanted to use these elements in Bless Me, Ultima?

✔ Use specific examples from the text?

Students are asked to write an analytical paragraph reflecting on the strengths and weaknesses of writing like an oral storyteller. Before they begin, make a list on the board of possible drawbacks that a writer might experience when trying to write in this fashion.

READING AND WRITING EXTENSIONS

➤ Ask students to use elements of the oral tradition to write about a significant event in their lives. Be sure they identify a storyteller and a listener within their text.

➤ Invite students to imagine what Antonio will be thinking about the next time he visits the river. Write an interior monologue for the boy as he stands on the bank of the river.

➤ The African-American culture is also rich in storytelling texts. Visit the school library to explore books by Virginia Hamilton (*The People Can Fly*) and Julius Lester.

Five Finding a Style

C r i t i c a l   R e a d i n g

FOCUS

Rudolfo Anaya on traditional values:

"I think one of the things we see going on in ... this country, perhaps in the world, is that what we call the old traditional cultures that were land-based and had a deep sense of legend and story and mythology and spiritual thought and ceremonies and dances are in the midst of change. They're being displaced. They're being pushed out."

BACKGROUND

Anaya is a writer committed to celebrating Chicano culture in his writing. Everything he writes is in some way a reflection of his heritage. Over the years he has developed a writing style that also reflects his pride in his ancestry. In Lesson Five, "Finding a Style," students are asked to consider Anaya's writing style. What are some of the characteristics that make his style unique? How is Anaya's voice a reflection of his culture?

➤ Notice the slow, even pace of Anaya's tone in his writing. He never hurries through a description just as he never hurries through a story. By his own admission, he tries to write as his *abuelo* lived his life: slowly, patiently, and peacefully.

➤ Another distinctive feature in Anaya's writing style is his use of Spanish. He punctuates his English texts with words and phrases from his own native tongue. This is another way of celebrating his heritage.

➤ Notice also Anaya's use of figurative language. His generous use of sensory details, similes, and imagery makes his writing come alive for readers whether or not they are familiar with the author's external or internal landscapes. Anaya is also known for his skillful use of extended metaphors (i.e., "An American Chicano in King Arthur's Court").

FOR DISCUSSION AND REFLECTION

Have students reflect on Anaya's writing style by having them choose passages from the three Anaya selections that struck them as particularly good writing. Discuss why the passages are examples of good writing.

➤ What elements of Anaya's style reflect his Chicano heritage? (Responses will vary.)

W r i t i n g

QUICK ASSESS

Do students:

✔ identify the different elements of Anaya's style?

✔ discuss the overall effect of this style?

✔ discuss the importance of tradition in Anaya's writing?

Students are asked to find in each of the three selections ("An American Chicano in ' King Arthur's Court," "A Celebration of Grandfathers," and the excerpt from *Bless Me, Ultima*) examples of key topics in Anaya's writing: the meeting of cultures, the importance of respect, the importance of the past, and awe in the beauty and mystery of the universe. They will then use this evidence to write a letter describing Anaya's writing style to someone who has never read his work.

READING AND WRITING EXTENSIONS

➤ Ask students to reread the second paragraph of "An American Chicano in King Arthur's Court." Then have them decide: does it seem that Anaya has followed his *curandera's* advice to "write what you know"?

➤ As a class make a list of 25 similes to describe Rudolfo Anaya's writing style. (For example, "Anaya's prose is like a golden carp moving slowly beneath the surface of a reader's brain; Anaya's stories are like visiting a place I have never been; Anaya's words are like spices on my tongue.")

Index

Teacher's guide pages numbers are in parentheses following pupil's edition page numbers.

Lesson Title Index

Literature Index